BIBLICAL
MISSIONARIES

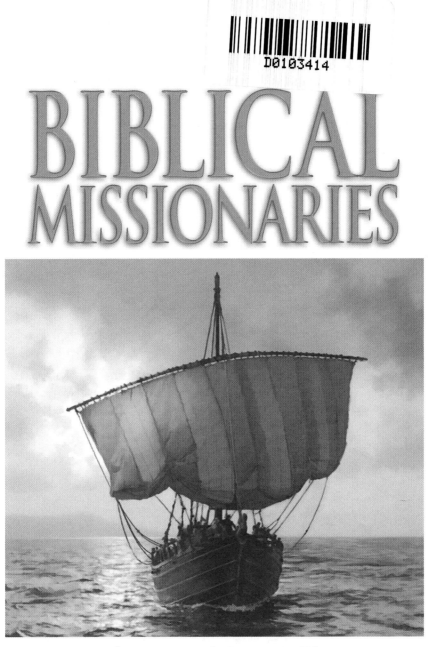

Børge Schantz and Steven Thompson

Pacific Press®
Publishing Association

Nampa, Idaho | Oshawa, Ontario, Canada
www.pacificpress.com

Cover design resources from Lars Justinen
Inside design by Kristin Hansen-Mellish

The authors assume full responsibility for the accuracy of all facts and quotations as cited in this book.

You can obtain additional copies of this book by calling toll-free 1-800-7656955 or by visiting http://www.adventistbookcenter.com.

Library of Congress Cataloging-in-Publication Data:
Thompson, Steven, 1947–
   Biblical missionaries / Steven Thompson and Borge Schantz.
      pages cm
   ISBN 13: 978-0-8163-5711-6 (pbk.)
   ISBN 10: 0-8163-5711-0 (pbk.)
1. Bible—Biography. 2. Missionaries. 3. Missions—Theory. 4. Seventh-day Adventists—Doctrines. I. Title.
   BS571.T47 2015
   220.9'2—dc23
                              2014040467

January 2015

Dedication

This book is dedicated to Adventist Sabbath School class members worldwide. Your attendance makes Sabbath School both a possibility and a blessing. May your Christian witness and service across the back fence, across the workbench, and across the cultural divides in your community be strengthened as you study the lives of biblical missionaries.

Contents

Introduction

When the God of the Bible had a special message for this world, He, on rare occasions, came in person to deliver it: "The Lord God, walking in the garden, . . . called to the man, 'Where are you?' " (Genesis 3:9).[1] At Mount Sinai, He told Moses, "I Myself will come to you covered in thick cloud so the people can hear Me" (Exodus 19:9). More frequently God sent an angel to deliver His messages.[2] The "angel of the Lord" or "angel of God" appears more than fifty times in the Old Testament, on God-assigned missions: "The angel of the Lord appeared to [Moses] in the leaping flames from the center of the bush" (Exodus 3:2). The angel of the Lord also came to Gideon (Judges 6), Samson's mother (Judges 13), and to several prophets including Elijah, Elisha, Daniel, and Zechariah (Zechariah 3:1–5). According to Ellen White, that angel "is Christ Himself, the Saviour of sinners."[3] God even used a talking donkey (Numbers 22) and stones (Habakkuk 2:11; Luke 19:40) as messengers!

But most often God sent humans to deliver His messages and carry out His tasks. These specially com*mission*ed biblical persons are rightly labeled as "missionaries" because they were sent on God's missions. The Latin word *missio,* meaning "the sending of persons; dispatching," is the source of the English word *mission.* From Genesis to Revelation, the Bible tells the stories of the biblical women, men, youth, and even children whom God sent on missions. Their mission stories make up one of the core strands of the Bible's overall message. Their successes and even their failings have served as inspiration, guidance, and caution through two thousand years of Christian mission.

Some of these biblical missionaries knew from the start exactly where God was sending them. He directed Jonah to "go to Nineveh, that great city" (Jonah 1:2, NKJV). He instructed Phillip to "go due south to the road from Jerusalem to Gaza" (Acts 8:26). But He sent others with little information about their destinations. All God told Abram was, "Go to the land I will show you" (Genesis 12:1).

Some were sent to people groups shockingly different from their own, requiring major cultural adjustments. The unnamed little Israelite girl must have puzzled why God allowed her to be captured and live in a foreign country as a servant to the wife of Naaman the Syrian. She could not know that she was a missionary in training. Daniel and his three companions, exiles in Babylon, refused food from the king's table in honor of their Hebrew faith. A few years later, Esther had to conceal her Jewish heritage and probably had to eat the foods that Daniel and his companions struggled to avoid, in order to carry out her unusual mission, including winning a nationwide beauty contest!

To prepare the apostle Peter to enter the Gentile home of Cornelius, commander of a dreaded Roman army unit, God sent a vision to Peter, telling him to kill and eat unclean animals (Acts 10:9–15). Saul of Tarsus, the strict Pharisee, was told, "I'm sending you to the Gentiles!" (Acts 26:17). While among those Gentiles, Peter and Paul had to translate the saving message of Jesus from the Jewish culture to the Gentile. As Paul later wrote, he lived like a Gentile, as part of becoming all things to all people, so that he might win them for Christ (1 Corinthians 9:19–23).

Long-distance travel was expected of some biblical missionaries. Paul wrote, "When I travel to Spain . . ." (Romans 15:24). Others were sent no farther than around the corner to immigrants and refugees struggling to settle into their adopted culture. Whether their journeys are geographical, cultural, or both, becoming missionaries takes people out of their comfort zones. Perhaps leaving one's comfort zone is a core requirement for every missionary.

Introduction

God's chief "Missionary" was His own Son, Jesus Christ—God's Word, who became flesh (see John 1:1–4, 9–14; 1 John 1:1–3). No missionary made a larger cultural transition (Colossians 1:15–17; Hebrews 2:14–18), left behind a greater comfort zone (Philippians 2:5–8), was more completely rejected and abandoned (Isaiah 53:3; Mark 14:50; John 1:10, 11; 1 Peter 2:4), or received more violent treatment (Matthew 27:22, 23; Hebrews 2:10) than Jesus. Yet no mission was more successful than His (Ephesians 2:14–18; Colossians 2:13–15; Hebrews 2:9; 1 Peter 1:18, 19).

God did not wait until biblical missionaries were perfect and fully trained. According to the German philosopher Immanuel Kant, "Out of the crooked timber of humanity no straight thing was ever made."[4] Despite their limitations—sometimes even because of them, as in the case of Abraham (chapter 2 in this book) and Jonah (chapter 4)—God chose, worked through, and blessed biblical missionaries as they carried out His missions. Even in their mistakes, poor decisions, and wrong actions, biblical missionaries demonstrate that the power of God can unite the most disparate and diverse individuals into harmonious teamwork, such as the case with Paul and Peter (Galatians 2:11–14). There is no better illustration of this than among the disciples of Jesus, who even during the Last Supper in the upper room were arguing who was the greatest (Luke 22:24–27). When they met again in an upper room after Jesus' resurrection, unity replaced rivalry as they prayed together (Acts 1:12–14) and received the Holy Spirit (Acts 2:4). Before that Day of Pentecost was over, the Christian church had been born, the first Christian sermon preached (verses 14–36), and the first Christian baptism conducted (verses 37–41). Christian mission had well and truly begun!

This study touches on the Bible's two mission models: the "come" model, in which the nations would come to God's people and learn of Him, and the "go" model, in which selected persons among God's people, such as Jonah and Paul, would go to surrounding nations. According to the "come" model, Israel was to be a prosperous and successful nation, a light on a hill to which the nations would come to learn of Israel's God and the blessings of living in harmony with His revealed will (Genesis 12:1–4; 1 Kings 8:41–43; 2 Chronicles 6:32, 33; Isaiah 56:6, 7; 61:8, 9).

Jesus Christ prepared His followers for the "go" model of mission: "Go therefore and make disciples of all nations" (Matthew 28:19, NKJV). His earliest followers moved in ever-expanding circles among the nations with the message that Jesus was God's Son, the promised Messiah and Savior of the world. This continues to be the main model of Christian mission.

The popular image of a Christian missionary during the colonial era was someone wearing a pith helmet who returned from many years in a distant land, telling exciting stories of jungles, dangerous animals, and exotic peoples and customs. This has been replaced by the postcolonial image of Christians devoting vacation time to short-term service trips, building and improving infrastructure, or providing short-term evangelism, education, or health care where there is special need. All are missionaries if they go in response to God's commission.

What about the majority of Christians who never go to a foreign mission field but stay home? Can they fulfill Jesus' gospel commission to "make disciples of all nations"? This question is answered partly in an unexpected Bible passage—the fourth commandment. This may seem to be an unlikely place for a mission statement. But the fourth commandment names a mission field that can be visited easily by nearly every Christian believer from their own home and local church: "The seventh day is the Sabbath of the Lord your God; in it you must not earn your living,[5] neither you nor your son or your daughter, nor your male or your female servant, nor your domestic animals, *nor your stranger who is within your gate*" (Exodus 20:10). Who is this "stranger"[6] within the "gate" of the Israelites? The best explanation occurs just three chapters later, where the Lord reminded the Israelites of their time as unprotected and exploited foreign settlers: "You were strangers in the land of Egypt" (Exodus 23:9, NKJV). The time would come, once the Israelites settled the Promised Land, that they would be approached by foreigners seeking refuge, shelter, and employment. While the fourth commandment called for an employment-free day each week for these immigrants, guest workers, and refugees, it also laid the foundation for witness. In today's Christian setting, this part of the fourth commandment calls on stay-at-home Christians to have their eyes opened to see these recent arrivals as opportunities for service and witness. Meeting their physical, economic, health, social, and spiritual needs will enable them to enjoy a Sabbath rest from their struggles to survive in our communities. It will also let them and their children see Christianity in action. This is part of God's mission.

The Bible's overall message is that mission is God's initiative: "Then I heard the voice of the Lord saying, 'Whom shall I send? And who will go for us?' " (Isaiah 6:8). God could once again, as of old, go Himself, because His mission of saving humans and restoring a safe, sinless, and sustainable world is of eternal importance (Isaiah 65:19–25; Revelation 21:1–5). But He continues to call and com*mission mission*aries. At the core of His mission plan is Jesus Christ, whose life, death, resurrection, current heavenly ministry, and soon return are central to every missionary's message. Only God can bring success to this mission, but He has chosen not to do it alone. He has made His mission dependent on His followers.

It is the hope and prayer of the author of the Sabbath School lessons for this quarter and the author of this book that by the quarter's end we will respond even more readily to God's next mission call to us: "Here I am, Lord; send me!" (Isaiah 6:8).

---

1. Unless otherwise noted, all Scriptures references in the introduction are the author's translation.

2. The Hebrew word *mal'āk*, usually translated "angel" focuses on the messenger role of heavenly, and sometimes earthly, beings.

3. E. G. White, *Counsels for the Church* (Nampa, ID: Pacific Press®, 1991), 350.

4. This aphorism has become known in English through British philosopher Isaiah Berlin's book, *The Crooked Timber of Humanity,* ed. Henry Hardy (London: John Murray, 1990).

5. The Hebrew noun *melākâ* translated "work" in Exodus 20:9, 10 occurs more than 160 times and is defined as "business, work, handiwork, craftsmanship, service." In other words, the way one earns one's living.

6. A Hebrew *gēr* is a settler who lacks the status and protection that comes with what we today think of as citizenship, and who often needs the help of citizens in order to survive and thrive in the adopted community.

The Missionary Nature of God

God's first earthly journey, according to the Bible, was a missionary journey—walking to and fro in the Garden of Eden and looking for the first man and woman. In response to their newly gained knowledge of good and evil, they were driven by guilt and shame to hide from their Creator. He found them and gently told them what would happen because of their choice to disobey. He also provided better covering for their nakedness than the leaves that they used. Most important, He promised them a future Deliverer (Genesis 3:8–15).

This was the first of several of God's "missionary journeys." Later, He stopped by Abraham's tent on His mission "walk" to Sodom (Genesis 18:1, 33). His journey had two purposes. He came to announce to Abraham and Sarah that the promised son would be born within a year. Then He intended to see for Himself and to know whether the complaints about the wickedness of Sodom were as bad as the cries that had reached Him suggested (verse 21). Later, King Solomon, in his prayer dedicating the newly built temple, praised God who "went out" (literally, "walked") to redeem for Himself His people Israel (1 Chronicles 17:21). According to the prophet Isaiah, Yahweh offered to walk ahead of King Cyrus of Persia as the king started out on his God-assigned mission to rescue Israel from Babylonian captivity (Isaiah 45:1–5).

Each of these passages employs the Hebrew verb *hālak*—meaning "to walk"—in order to present God in mission mode, on the move, leading a search-and-rescue operation to recover fallen humans. When the risen Jesus ordered His disciples to "go into all the world and preach the gospel to all creation" (Mark 16:15), His choice of language was probably influenced by these Old Testament references to God's own missionary endeavors.

God created man and woman and gave them moral freedom

But why would God, who created a world that He pronounced "very good," need to visit it and undertake a search-and-rescue mission?

To understand this need, one needs to review important parts of the Bible story of the creation of humanity. The lesson for Sunday lists seven points about the creation of man and woman that set them apart from the other living creatures. The message of the Bible is that God intended to relate to people in a relationship based on love.

> God, according to the Bible, possesses personhood and is the source of all personhood, including my own. Key attributes of human personhood include the will, individuality, a sense of differentiation, and the capacity to form relationships. The Bible attributes these to God, and repeatedly records human interaction with Him in relational terms. No part of the Bible is free from the language of relationship; it dominates the books of Moses, the Psalms, the prophets, the New Testament letters and especially the teaching of Jesus. The God of the Bible intends to relate.[1]

The overall message is that man and woman stand somewhat separate from other living beings and have a closer, more complex relationship to God. Special qualities God gave them, such as His image and likeness, suited them for their responsibility to have dominion over the rest of creation and to produce offspring who would populate the earth as God directed. They and the earth over which they had dominion were expected to remain "very good." In order to make this possible, God gave the man and woman freedom to make choices.

Are humans really free to make choices, moral choices especially? Or are they programmed, locked into what God, or nature, or the stars decide for them? The reality of free will has been debated through history.

From the Bible's viewpoint, there is no debate. The answer is yes! Humans are free to make real choices, including the choice for or against salvation. This truth is seen in the fact that the Lord God gave the first man and woman freedom to make a real choice in the Garden of Eden. A careful reading of Genesis 3:1–13 shows the man and woman freely making that choice.

That people have free will has been, and remains, the Seventh-day Adventist understanding of human nature. Ellen White wrote:

> God might have created man without the power to transgress His law; he might have withheld the hand of Adam from touching the forbidden fruit; but in that case man would have been, not a free moral agent, but a mere automaton. Without freedom of choice, his obedience would not have been voluntary, but forced.[2]

The author of this quarter's Sabbath School lessons, missiologist Børge Schantz, has restated the Adventist position on the reality of free will: "Men and women were endowed with free will. This means that the Creator will not assert his power over the desires and choices of human individuals."[3] Freedom of the human can exist because God has taken upon Himself certain limitations in order to grant to humans the significant freedom to which Genesis testifies. "God took a risk by limiting himself. The immediate negative result of this limitation was the Fall."[4] What this means for salvation is that just as it "was an exercise of man's use of his free will that brought separation between God and man . . . it will also need an exercise of free will to regain the status men and women lost in the original Garden of Eden."[5]

God loses man and woman

God's close relationship to the man and woman meant that when they chose to disobey Him, He also had to make choices, including the hard choice to do what He had stated—send them out of the Garden and ban them from returning. God's relationship with humans was hugely set back by the Fall. In order for God to restore it, a plan formed "from the foundation of the world" (an expression that occurs ten times in the New Testament, mostly referring to God's saving mission) was put into action. It involved all persons of the Godhead—Father, Son, and Holy Spirit—who worked in unity to restore the damaged relationship.

All good relationships need care and nurture. Damaged ones need even more of that care and nurture to bring the relationship back to health and strength. Perhaps this is reflected in the Bible's stories that show how many differing forms of communication and relationship God has used. It is also reflected in God's unwillingness to "give up," even when people ignored His offer to relate: "Can a mother forget the baby at her breast and have no compassion on the child she has borne? Though she may forget, I will not forget you!" (Isaiah 49:15).

While the story of the Fall in Genesis 3 is well known, it should be read again, keeping in mind the freedom of choice revealed there. Read the story carefully, one verse at a time. Try to answer the question, What choices did the woman or the man make in this verse? A large number of real choices will come to the attention of readers who follow this suggestion.

God's initiative to save humanity

God's Old Testament "saving walks" mentioned above give small glimpses of His initiative to save men and women from life and death in a fallen world. His plan to save became the central focus and message of the Bible. Not only of God the Father, but also of the entire Godhead—Father, Son, and Holy Spirit—united in a saving mission.

The mission would center on the person, the life, and the work of Jesus Christ.

The heart of [God's] plan has been sacrificially to give His own divine Son to come and be one with us as a man to show us what godly love is really all about. The climax of the Son's mission was to live and die in such a way that we could be forgiven, reconciled, and ultimately healed of the disease of sin.[6]

Wednesday's lesson points out the cluster of special qualities that made it possible for Jesus to reunite fallen humans with God. He was both God and human; both Judge, Advocate, and Savior of the world.

But the divine "missionary team" would not be complete without the Holy Spirit, who, on the Day of Pentecost, birthday of the Christian Church, brought the holy fire and wind that changed the shocked disciples into a powerful team of eyewitnesses who would do their part for world mission. It was on that day the Holy Spirit gave a clear message to the infant Christian church that its mission message and target people were changing. In that upper room on that day, the praise of God was heard in multiple languages in order to prepare believers for taking the gospel to the world. No longer was its focus to be restricted to a single ethnic group.

The expression "salvation history," which is found on the Sabbath afternoon page of this week's lesson, is better known among Seventh-day Adventists as the "plan of redemption." This was a favorite expression of Seventh-day Adventist pioneer and spiritual leader Ellen G. White. It is found more than 150 times in her published writings.[7] It is like a cord that runs through her five-volume Conflict of the Ages series, and it is summarized in *The Story of Redemption*.[8]

She understood God's plan of redemption, or salvation history, to be the message of both the Old and New Testaments. From Genesis to Revelation, the individual stories, prophecies, promises, warnings, and revelations fit together as the many parts of God's saving work for fallen humanity. For her, the center of salvation history was the birth, ministry, crucifixion, and resurrection of Jesus Christ and His ongoing heavenly ministry. She longed to see the next step of salvation history, Christ's second coming—His personal, visible return to this earth at the end of the age to collect all who have accepted His invitation and placed their faith in Him.

He's got the whole world in His hands—and in His plans!

Those earliest believers on, and just after, the Day of Pentecost, who received the outpouring of the Holy Spirit, would soon face an ethnic issue that challenged their ability to carry out the gospel commission. In their ears were still ringing the words of Jesus' commission: "This gospel of the kingdom will be preached in *the whole world* as a witness to *all nations*" (Matthew 24:14, author's translation). "God so loved *the world* that he gave his one and only Son" (John 3:16, emphasis added).

All of the earliest Christians were Jews. Their cultural, ethnic, and religious upbringing put barriers between them and the rest of the world's people groups. How would they break through these ethnic and religious barriers in order to reach every tribe and nation and kindred and people? How would they shift from what this week's lesson terms a "light" pattern of mission, where God's people shine like a light and attract others to come to them and learn of God, to a "salt" pattern of mission, in which mission workers are scattered thinly, like salt spread through the nations?

God gave the answer on the Day of Pentecost. He placed it in Peter's Pentecost sermon, at the point where Peter quoted the Old Testament prophet Joel's record of God's amazing assertion, "I will pour out my Spirit on *all people*" (Joel 2:28, emphasis added). The Lord here promised the Spirit to all people—a promise backed up in verse 32: "*Everyone* who calls on the name of the LORD will be saved" (emphasis added). Peter could have (and probably did) quote additional Old Testament prophecies that pointed ahead to the time when the good news of God's search-and-rescue mission would extend to all the world's inhabitants.

Conclusion

The biblical picture of God, from Genesis to Revelation, focuses on His initiative in finding and saving His people. He came to Adam and Eve, He came to Abram, and He came to live with His people of Israel in the sanctuary. The theme of the coming God is repeated across the Old Testament and especially into the New, in the ministry of Jesus Christ. Even in the New Testament, however, the coming God Himself is still expected—" 'I am the Alpha and the Omega,' says the Lord

God, 'who is and who was *and who is to come*' " (Revelation 1:8, emphasis added). Today, God comes to people groups of this world through the persons of His followers. Through them God continues to "walk" among the nations, using the feet of His human agents. He demonstrates His unfailing love for all humanity through the ministry, crucifixion, resurrection, and heavenly ministry of Jesus Christ. He appeals to human hearts today through the presence of the Holy Spirit. He will send His Son Jesus Christ back to this earth at the end of this age to rescue all who have turned to Him. In the meantime, God still recruits humans, including us, to share His mission. This is the theme of this series of Sabbath School lessons.

1. Steven Thompson, "Who Is God? What Is He Like?" in Michael Westacott and John Ashton, eds., *The Big Argument: Does God Exist?* (Sydney: Strand Publishing, 2005), 242.

2. Ellen G. White, *Patriarchs and Prophets* (Mountain View, CA: Pacific Press®, 1958), 49.

3. Børge Schantz, "The Limitation of God and the Free Will and Holy Ignorance of Man: Towards an Understanding of the Plight of the Un-warned," in Børge Schantz and Reinder Bruinsma, eds., *Exploring the Frontiers of Faith: Festschrift in Honour of Dr. Jan Paulsen* (Lueneburg, Germany: Advent-Verlag, 2009), 405.

4. Ibid., 406.

5. Ibid., 406, 407.

6. Woodrow Whidden, Jerry Moon, and John W. Reeve, *The Trinity: Understanding God's Love, His Plan of Salvation, and Christian Relationships* (Hagerstown, MD: Review and Herald®, 2002), 249.

7. Ellen G. White Estate, *Comprehensive Index to the Writings of Ellen G. White* (Mountain View, CA: Pacific Press®, 1962), 2:2066–2069.

8. Ellen G. White, *The Story of Redemption* (Washington, DC: Review and Herald®, 1947).

Abraham:
The First Missionary

"Consider Abraham," the apostle Paul urged his readers (see Galatians 3:6). This was possible for them, as it is for us, because Abraham's story spreads across fourteen chapters of the book of Genesis, and his name occurs in the Old Testament 216 times.[1] His spiritual footprints stride beyond the Jewish people and extend into the world of the early Christians, with more than seventy-five occurrences of his name in the New Testament. He is also highly significant for Islam, where he is mentioned in thirty-five chapters of the Koran, more than any other biblical figure except Moses.[2] The Genesis stories contain inspired insights that will enhance our understanding of Abraham's human characteristics, his unique mission, and his well-deserved place as God's first missionary.

The key spiritual reality of Abraham's life, which placed him in his central role in the world's three monotheist faiths, was his staunch belief that there is only one true God. He also believed that this one God had singled him out from within his polytheistic Chaldean culture, had directly addressed him, and had sent him on a special journey, a mission. This conviction energized his lifetime commitment to his mission, steadying him and sustaining him during some of the personal,

23

cultural, and spiritual struggles he encountered as a prototype and example for future missionaries.

The call of Abraham

The Lord's first recorded direct communication to this future pioneer missionary for monotheism was: "Go from your country, your people and your father's household to the land I will show you" (Genesis 12:1). The original Hebrew text is a little more blunt. It can be translated "You! Start walking!" God's instructions, plus His promise of future blessing, started the first human missionary on his way. "So Abram went, as the Lord had told him" (verse 4).

The Lord's command to "start walking" was not open-ended. It had a goal. Abram was directed to walk *away from* his country, his extended family, and his immediate family (verse 1). He was to walk *toward* an undisclosed destination, which the Lord would eventually show him, but only after Abram was well into his walk. At the beginning "he did not know where he was going" (Hebrews 11:8). Faith in the Lord's promise, rather than knowledge of his destination, marked Abram's core spiritual orientation and enabled him to take that huge initial countercultural step demanded of missionaries: leaving country, family, and home.

Facing foreign customs

Abraham's mission journey started in his seventy-fifth year, a time when most have settled into retirement. He traveled in two foreign countries, Canaan and Egypt, where customs and beliefs sometimes were a threat to his mission effectiveness. Both cultures often challenged his faith. Even the climate, with its repeated droughts and famines, sometimes threatened that faith. Later, Abraham's Hebrew descendants were reminded how serious those days were in Abram's journey. Every time they presented their offering of firstfruits, at a certain place in the ceremony they recited about Abraham, "An Aramean on the point of death [was] my [fore]father, and he went down into Egypt as a refugee" (Deuteronomy 26:5).[3]

The Old Testament expression "famine in the land"[4] prepares the reader for a look at a harsh fact of life in the land of Canaan. The Hebrew word translated "famine" occurs 101 times in the Old Testament, 24 of them in Genesis. Three famines threatened Abram and his descendants: the first one in Genesis 12; another during the days of Isaac in Genesis 26; and a third in Joseph's time, starting in the forty-first chapter. Abram's response to the famine was to "go down to Egypt." The Old Testament expression "go down [to such-and-such a place]" became an expression for pain and loss (see Genesis 39:1; Numbers 20:15; Isaiah 52:4; Jeremiah 30:3; 31:1). According to Scripture, neither Abram nor his descendants would do well in Egypt. Their time in Egypt brought them difficulty and suffering.

Egypt posed a real and serious danger to Abram's family. There his wife Sarai was taken from him, just as he expected might happen. In order to have a better chance of surviving, he agreed with her, before they entered Egypt, to tell a half-truth about their relationship (Genesis 12:13). It was true that Sarai was Abram's half-sister as well as his wife, as he later said (Genesis 20:12).

But a half-truth about a relationship so fundamental as marriage was wrong. According to the revealed will of God (Genesis 2:24), and even according to the laws of Abram's home country, marriage had a visible and public side as well as a private side.[5] Abram knew better, and he deserved the Lord's rebuke, spoken through the Pharaoh, for hiding such an important truth about Sarai.

The Hebrew word *gūr,* meaning "to live as a resident alien; take refuge as a refugee," occurs in Genesis 12:10 so the reader understands that Abram not only *went down* to Egypt, but he also had the legal status there of resident alien. As resident aliens, he and his family risked exploitation in Egypt's very ethnocentric culture. The date usually assigned to Abram, about 2000 B.C., places his Egyptian sojourn during that country's twelfth dynasty. It was well known for its antiforeigner talk and laws. Archaeologists have learned of this through curses against neighboring peoples written on clay bowls and small clay human figures. They were probably used in public religious rituals to call on Egypt's gods to protect the country against "foreigners." These texts curse immigrants from Canaan, including those from Jerusalem and

Shechem, a city Abram visited, according to Genesis 12:6. Today, multiple millions—more than at any time since 1945—around the world live as refugees in foreign countries where every day they face dangers and hardships.

Facing a severe famine in Canaan, Abram felt he had little choice. He reckoned that risking his life as a refugee in Egypt was better than starving in Canaan. Travel and survival in both Canaan and Egypt called for resilience, faith, and fortitude, especially while he was struggling to keep his wife and family safe and intact. And Abram learned the hard way about honesty and trust in God when declaring the truth about relationships.

Abraham's wealth: Divine blessing or troublesome excess baggage?

The way Abram related to wealth—his own, and that of other people—enters the biblical story. Before Abram left Egypt, Pharaoh generously paid him for the short-term loss of Sarai. He received seven types of gifts, all of them alive, including humans (Genesis 12:16). Genesis 13:1 adds "silver and gold" to the list of Abram's goods. He left Egypt a rich man.

There are some cases, as later missionaries have learned, where material goods can be a burden rather than a blessing. Relationships and efforts to witness can come under stress where there is a gap between those who have these goods and those who do not. That was Abram's experience. His goods probably helped cause a breakup of his extended family, which later brought his nephew Lot into danger in Sodom (Genesis 13:5–13). Abram would later rescue Lot. By doing so, he showed that he had learned the importance of his future role of bringing a blessing to all the families of the earth (Genesis 12:3).

Abraham's testimony to ten kings about family and goods

Some people believe wealth was one of the seven promises the Lord made to Abram when He called him and promised to "bless" him (Genesis 12:1–3). But "blessing" here and other places in Genesis more likely refers to God's gift of family and children. Abram seems to have learned a lesson about the trouble wealth brought on his extended family. God later used Abram as a witness about the importance of family, compared to the importance of goods (Genesis 14:21–24).

Abram was enjoying country living on the plain of Mamre when, one day, someone who had been captured in Sodom was able to escape and bring the bad news that Abram's nephew Lot had been taken captive, along with many others from Sodom (Genesis 14:13). This opened up a new form of mission for Abram, but he had prepared for trouble by arming more than three hundred men from his family and his workers and servants. With God's help they caught up with the war captives at Dan and rescued them. Abram put himself and some of his immediate family in danger in order to rescue another part of his family. This was powerful testimony that impressed the king of Sodom.

Abram testified in a second way to the king of Sodom when, after a successful battle, he rescued the captives and recovered their goods from the invading armies. When the priest and king of Salem, Melchizedek, arrived with bread and wine to thank God for Abram's victory, Abram paid him tithe: "a tenth of everything" (verse 20).

Abram's third testimony before the king of Sodom was his refusal—after rescuing his nephew Lot and the other captives, along with their goods, and paying tithe—to take a share of the remaining goods for himself. This went against custom, which allowed the victors in battle to take a share of the recovered goods (verses 21–24). Abram testified to the king his reason for refusing: he had taken a solemn oath, with hand raised to God, to refuse any property—even a piece of sewing thread or a sandal thong—that belonged to anyone else (verse 22). He explained the motive behind his oath: "Lest you should say, 'I have made Abram rich!' " (verse 23, ESV). As a missionary Abram came to spiritually enrich people, not to exploit them in any way or profit by their loss. This refusal of further enrichment was also powerful testimony to the king of Sodom about the character of Abram's God.

Another part of Abram's mission appears in his practice of building altars and calling on the name of his God. He built at least three altars[6] and called on the name of the Lord at least three times.[7] These public actions testified to the local peoples about Abram's faith.

The effect of ethnic prejudice

The need to generalize is planted deeply within most people and not easily switched off. Generalizations can be useful. For example, "Cars always come down that hill too fast!" But when applied to people groups, generalizations can be unfair and wrong about members of those groups, as in "Americans are all alike. All they want to do is _____!" (Fill in the blank.) Abram generalized about Egyptians before entering their country: "They will kill me!" (Genesis 12:12). It did not happen; the Egyptians "treated Abram well" (verse 16). Abram's generalization showed an even deeper ethnic prejudice as he entered Gerar territory: "There is *for certain* no fear of God in this place!" (Genesis 20:11, author's translation).[8] Again he was wrong. Instead of being killed in Gerar, he was welcomed. He, and later his son Isaac, found Gerar safe and pleasant, and they decided to sojourn there (Genesis 20:1; 26:2, 6).

Must missionaries be morally superior?

Does God choose and send only missionaries who have higher moral standards than the people they serve? Some Christians, brought up on traditional mission stories, have this image of a one-way flow of truth *from* the missionary *to* the target people. But two of Abram's experiences point to a two-way teaching—sometimes the missionary is the humble learner sitting at the feet of the target people instead of the other way around.

Two times the people to whom Abram was sent had something to teach him about honesty and truth speaking. Both times Abram concealed the fact of his marriage to Sarai. Both times his dishonesty was named and openly rebuked by a pagan king. In Egypt, Pharaoh asked Abram why he was not truthful: "Why didn't you tell me she was your wife? Why did you say, 'She is my sister'?" (Genesis 12:18).

Later, in Gerar, God revealed Abram's dishonesty in a dream to King Abimelech, who then said to Abram, "You have done things to me that should never be done" (Genesis 20:9). Even though both Pharaoh and Abimelech probably worshiped idols and lacked knowledge of the God of Abram, they both knew about honesty and truth-telling through natural law—what Paul referred to as the law written on the heart (Romans 2:13–15; read also 1:19, 20). Although these incidents predated the giving of the ninth commandment at Mount Sinai ("You shall not bear false witness" [Exodus 20:16, NKJV]), those pagan kings knew about right and wrong. It was they, not Abram, who called for a higher moral standard.

Abraham: Wandering missionary-reformer

A wise pastor once stated, "Travel broadens a person." Sometimes people need to "get away from home" in order to be freed from family spirits and traditions they would otherwise not be able to resist. Some people travel to find themselves. Abram traveled to find God. Speaking through Joshua, God later reminded the Israelites of this truth: "Long ago your ancestors, including Terah the father of Abraham and Nahor, lived beyond the Euphrates River and worshiped other gods. But I took your father Abraham from the land . . . and led him" (Joshua 24:2, 3). The lesson for Wednesday invites readers to review the stories of Abram's "spiritual high points" in five places where he sojourned.

Journeys differ in one important way from pilgrimages. While journeys do not need to have a destination, pilgrimages do. It is possible for people to begin a journey with no destination in mind. Pilgrims start a pilgrimage with a very clear destination as their goal. Every step hopefully takes them toward it, even if they have to detour and make adjustments on the way. Did God lead Abram on a journey or a pilgrimage?

Abraham: Missionary in his own house

The pastor who said, "Travel broadens a person" finished his statement by adding, "but it doesn't deepen them."

Though personal broadening takes place on the pilgrimage, the best place for personal and spiritual deepening may be at home. Although Abraham met many trials, and failed some, as head of the household he became a deeper person. In the New Testament's summary of the main events in his life, the following stand out: "Abraham . . . obeyed . . . made his home in the promised land . . . was looking forward to the city . . . whose architect and builder is God . . . was enabled to bear

29

children . . . offered [up] Isaac" (Hebrews 11:8–17). Note that most of these took place "at home." God repeatedly lifted his hope of becoming a father during those long years of Sarah's childlessness. When the promised son arrived, Abraham's faith sustained him through the most terrible thing a father can imagine—sacrificing that son. Could it be that his greatest victories and his most humbling failures took place in his home or with members of his own family?

Mission and ministry are the cause of stress as well as of blessing for the families of all who answer the call. The wreckage of the failed families of Christian workers is clearly visible. Through the testing and turmoil, Abraham emerged from seeming family failure as a caring father—not only of Ishmael and Isaac but also of an entire people. His struggling but growing fatherly commitment to his own family laid the foundation for his eventual role as "father of a multitude," as indicated by his change of name from Abram to Abraham (Genesis 17:5). And for his many spiritual children he is also father of mission.

This week's lesson closes by reminding readers of the large, rich, and varied "family" of Abraham, who became and remains biological "father" of Arabs and Jews and spiritual "father" of Christians and Muslims even today. His faith and his obedience continue to inspire mission and missionaries to this day.

---

1. According to a Biblegateway.com search of NIV, "Abram," 57 occurrences, "Abraham," 159 occurrences.

2. Francis E. Peters, *Islam: A Guide for Jews and Christians* (Princeton, NJ: Princeton University Press, 2003), 9. One chapter of the Koran, Surah 14, bears his name.

3. My own translation. For support, see *The Dictionary of Classical Hebrew* (Sheffield, England: Sheffield Academic Press, 1993), 1:99.

4. Genesis 12:10; 26:1; 42:5; 47:4; Ruth 1:1; 2 Samuel 24:13; Ezekiel 34:29; Amos 8:11; Psalm 105:16.

5. The famous law code of King Hammurabi of Babylon, although dated about two hundred years after Abraham's time, focuses on marriage in fifty of its 282 surviving clauses (numbers 127 to 177).

6. See Genesis 12:7; 13:18; 22:9.

7. See Genesis 12:8; 13:4; 21:33.

8. My own translation of "for certain" brings out the meaning of Hebrew *raq,* which has affirmative force: "certainly," "surely."

CHAPTER

Naaman: Syrian Military Commander With Leprosy

Is it wrong for a believer to aid an enemy of his or her people? This question meets readers of the story of Naaman, Israel's enemy, in 2 Kings 5.

David became king of Judah and then of Israel about 1000 B.C. He quickly conquered Syria, including its capital city, Damascus (see 2 Samuel 8:6). Damascus broke free of Israel's control when Rezon of Syria staged a successful independence struggle during the reign of David's son, Solomon. For this reason Rezon remained "an adversary of Israel" (1 Kings 11:25, ESV).[1] About three generations later, during the reign of King Ahab (about 875–853 B.C.), the Syrians were still sending raiding parties into Israel (2 Kings 5:2).

During one of these raids a little Israelite girl was captured and brought back to Syria. Her name is not recorded. She, like the unnamed Samaritan woman whom Jesus met centuries later (see John 4), shared her faith before fading quietly from Scripture. Her witness had lasting results. While working as a servant to Naaman's wife, she told her mistress there was a man of God, a prophet in Israel, who could heal Naaman's leprosy.

Naaman, Syrian general

The model of Christian mission that many have grown up with is that of missionaries from the more prosperous developed countries serving in less prosperous ones. There they meet basic human needs as an avenue to meeting people's deeper spiritual needs. Naaman does not fit this pattern. He had money, power, and connections. He lived in or near Damascus, a cultured and prosperous city known for the valuable products of its merchants, including excellent wine produced in its vineyards (Ezekiel 27:16–18). The Abana River (now named Barada) provided a year-round water supply. The soil of the region was fertile. Its reputation in the ancient world nearly matched that of Israel, "the land of milk and honey."

As commander of the Syrian army, Naaman was Israel's public enemy number one. He would have given the orders, after all, for those commando raids on Israelite towns. After the capture of the little Israelite girl, Naaman must have become personal enemy number one to her family of origin. His orders that led to her kidnapping took her away from home, family, and a chance to grow up among her people and religion.

What can this story teach about conducting Christian mission with persons in high office, in politically sensitive international settings, and even during times of war?

"But he had leprosy"

"But he had leprosy" (2 Kings 5:1).[2] Naaman's leprosy soured every part of his life. It stopped him enjoying the company of people who would otherwise be honored by the company of the commander in chief. It could not be healed by medicine, money, or power. This highly visible and socially isolating disease was with him every moment. It held him back at work, in public, and at home.[3] Was it the personal and social loneliness of Naaman that made him open to the servant girl's message about the life-changing power of God?

Contact persons: Servant girl, wife, two kings

The little Israelite "servant-missionary" to Naaman had not been commissioned and then sent off with fervent prayers and supported from the home field. Rather, she was a captive, possibly handpicked by Naaman as a personal servant for his wife. She spent her days "facing" her mistress.[4] Her long, humble, and probably tiring daily routine is echoed in a line from Psalm 123:2, "look[ing] to the hand of her mistress," alert to the slightest motion that would send her to her next chore. But this unnamed Israelite girl brought the good news of healing to Israel's main national enemy. She did this without any promise that the healed and restored Naaman would change his attitude toward Israel, Israel's people, or Israel's God.

When the time was right, the little girl's faithful service day after day must have impressed Naaman's wife and opened her mind to believe the girl's simple testimony: "If only master would 'face' the prophet who is in Samaria [capital city of Israel], he would separate him from his sickness!" (2 Kings 5:3, author's translation). These few words, numbering just ten in Hebrew, are the only ones to reach us from this captive child. But they started a train of events that would affect Naaman, his family, his nation, Israel, and thousands of Bible readers ever since.

Two kings assist in mission

Naaman's wife shared the girl's testimony with him. He passed it to the king of Damascus, who wrote a letter to the king of Israel. Naaman, filled with hope and with letter in hand, rode westward in his chariot.

Communication between national leaders sometimes hits the headlines, especially during times of international tension. Leaders and their advisors needed diplomatic skills to avoid misunderstanding. It sometimes helped to communicate using the services of neutral nations. Leaders who misunderstood or overreacted to messages from other leaders could start wars. The suspicious response of Israel's King Joram to the Syrian king's letter showed the high level of distrust between Israel and Syria.

According to 2 Kings 5:7, Joram read into the letter two messages that were not there. First, he applied the request for healing entirely to himself: "Am I God? Can I kill and bring back to life?" He next read a threat into it: "See how he is trying to pick a quarrel with me!" His reaction went public when he tore his royal robe, an action stated three times in verses 7 and 8. This was a public signal: he saw behind that letter a threat to his nation. Today's equivalent would be "going to the media" with an issue for which the government wanted publicity. This publicity brought the letter to the attention of the prophet Elisha.

As a result of King Joram "going public," many Israelites heard that the Syrian commander Naaman had come to Israel to be healed. How did God expect them to respond if Elisha, Israel's chief prophet-healer, healed such a high-ranking enemy? Did God have a place in the plan of salvation for Naaman and his people? Would Israel as God's chosen nation put national security into God's hands, freeing them to cooperate in this opportunity for witness by allowing Elisha to heal Naaman? How should they respond if this proved to be a sincere plea for help? After all, God's will and intention for Israel was for them to share their light with their neighbors: "Nations will come to your light and kings to the brightness of your dawn" (Isaiah 60:3). How should they respond to Naaman's plea?

Speaking truth to power

Naaman and his attendants were allowed to travel from the palace to Elisha's home. There, Elisha had to "speak the truth to power"—in this case, to a powerful enemy commander.

Pastor Barry Black, chaplain to the United States Senate, recently declared, "If you're going to prepare for a miracle where leprosy disappears, you've got to speak the truth to power."[5] Elisha was aware that powerful people need to hear the truth just as badly as do the rest.

The truth Naaman needed at that moment was that he needed to acknowledge the true God and to obey Him. So Elisha spoke truth in the form of brief instructions. He didn't even greet Naaman at the door, but let him stand outside, without the "face to face" of the servant girl (2 Kings 5:3). The prophet instead sent an unnamed messenger, who thus became a second "servant-missionary" used by God to "speak truth to power." Why did Elisha not come to the door himself and deal directly with Naaman? The story does not explain why. The lesson for Tuesday lists five possible reasons but leaves the reader to choose.

Elisha's unnamed messenger brought instructions to Naaman that could turn his life around. Two simple acts were all God required. First, he had to *walk* to the river Jordan instead of continuing in his chariot (verse 9).[6] Second, he had to *bathe* in it seven times. If Naaman obeyed, Elisha promised a double result. First, his body would be restored to childlike health; second, he would be regarded as cleansed from his disease—what we think of today as a certificate declaring a person free from a serious infectious disease (verse 10). Naaman had to decide.

Would he, commander in chief, submit to these instructions and do these humble actions?

Naaman's first response was emotional—"He became angry and walked away in hot anger" (verse 11, author's translation). Behind his emotions and more important to him was his freedom to choose. However Naaman may have *felt,* he was fully free to *make a choice* between following or not following instructions. Behind that was his freedom to believe or not to believe in the offer of healing by the God of Elisha.

This was the real choice facing Naaman. It was real because his will was free enough to make real choices. His life was not locked into an unchangeable pattern of cause and effect. His life was not controlled by fate or by the stars. Now was his time to act. His earlier belief in the little Israelite girl's testimony had been strong enough to bring him into enemy territory, into the palaces of the kings of two warring nations. It had brought him to the home of Elisha. Would it now get him, on foot, the eighteen miles (twenty-nine kilometers) to the Jordan River?

As Naaman stalked away in anger, his attendants stepped up to him and also spoke the truth to power (verse 13). They appealed to his soldier nature, which would not have flinched or hesitated if asked to do something hard. They soothed Naaman's emotions enough to allow his power of choice to take over. He followed Elisha's instructions by walking to the Jordan, where he bathed seven times and was healed. The results were spectacular—exactly what Elisha said would happen.

But the story did not end there.

Gracious commander and noble prophet

With his attendants, Naaman returned to Elisha's door (verse 15), this time to testify with great enthusiasm to the healing power of Israel's

God, the only true God. Naaman also came to pay for his healing, which is just what the healers connected to his own god back in Damascus would have expected. But Elisha turned down Naaman's silver, gold, and clothing.

This must have seemed very strange to Naaman. After all, even prophets needed to replace their clothing from time to time. And some of that gold and silver would come in handy, because Elisha would soon have to relocate and expand the school of the prophets, due to overcrowding (2 Kings 6:1–7). How much easier the rebuilding of the school would have been, and how much bigger, had he accepted that payment and used it for the new school.

But Elisha refused. He wanted Naaman to understand that the true God did not heal for pay. Unlike other gods, He did not do "fair exchange" transactions—"I heal you, you pay Me, then we're even and settled; no further obligations on either side." God wanted Naaman's heart, not his wealth. In the words of Elisha, "Is this the time to take money, or to accept clothes?" (2 Kings 5:26). Only when Elisha turned down the payment did this important truth about the God of Israel become clear to Naaman. His next two requests showed that he wanted to correctly worship his newly discovered God.

How does one worship God outside one's own territory? Naaman understood gods to be territorial; that is, each tribe, each city had its own god, whose powers faded as soon as they left their own territory. Probably this was in Naaman's mind when he asked for a two-mule load of Israelite dirt to take back to Damascus, so the true God would have a base in the heart of the Syrian god Rimmon's territory.

Holy dirt, holy water, holy bones, even souvenir pebbles from the spot where David killed Goliath, or olive wood from the Mount of Olives—all these carry special meaning for many people. Babies born to the royal families in the Scandinavian countries to this day are baptized in water from the Jordan River.

Naaman also asked permission to enter the temple of Rimmon from time to time as part of his official duties with his king. Elisha's only reply was, "Go in peace!" (2 Kings 5:19). He sensed by Naaman's request that God's Spirit was already working on his understanding as well as his heart. He believed Naaman's conversion was genuine, and that the commander would grow in knowledge at the pace God would set. A drastic, sudden change of belief and lifestyle might isolate Naaman from king, family, and friends, the very people God wanted to reach through him. Elisha also knew that back home, under Naaman's own roof, the little Israelite servant girl would help the "convert" to grow in knowledge of the one true God, the Creator and Redeemer, whose power reached "every nation, tribe, language and people" (Revelation 14:6).

What a wonderful story. It really *should* have ended here, but did not. Yet one more chapter was needed.

Dishonest servant

Gehazi had been, and continued to be, Elisha's long-term personal attendant. He was at Elisha's side at both high and low points in the prophet's encounters with the woman of Shunem (2 Kings 4:8–37; 8:1–6). When the Syrian army tried to capture Elisha by surrounding the city of Dothan, Gehazi was Elisha's attendant (2 Kings 6:15–17). It is possible he was one of the four lepers who later discovered that the Syrian army surrounding Samaria had been frightened away by God, leaving everything behind in their camp (2 Kings 6:24–7:20).[7] After he and his fellow lepers ate their fill of Syrian army food, they took and hid silver, gold, and clothing—the very items Naaman offered as pay. Soon afterward they acknowledged the selfishness of their actions (verse 9).

Gehazi wanted Naaman to pay for his healing. Perhaps the Syrians had attacked his own family and he now wanted compensation. Or maybe he was unable to resist a surge of greed when he saw the silver and gold. Gehazi's request for payment, falsely using the name of his master Elisha, was dishonest and disappointing, especially for someone so close to the prophet. In the words of one student of this story, "How desperate the failure in the prophet's own house!"[8] This ending to the story reminds readers of God's high standards of conduct, especially when involved in mission—and that should include all Christians at all times.

Conclusion

This week's study makes clear that mission does not fit a single pattern. Sometimes the only mission work possible is done by hardworking laypersons whose witness is made believable because of their excellent and faithful, everyday service. In the Christian era also, mission has been conducted by captive Christian girls and women who witnessed while they served. The names of a few are known, such as Rhipsime of Armenia and Theognosta of Georgia.[9] But the names of most have not survived. Like the little Israelite girl, only God knows their identities.

God can work through "servant-missionaries" when political and social tensions prevent regular missionary work. Also, God's plan for mission continues even when missionaries make serious mistakes. Finally, this week's study shows how even a "little" missionary can start something that leads to big results. Due to the simple testimony of a kidnapped Israelite servant girl, plus the timely words of other servant-missionaries, the Syrian commander Naaman was healed and converted. Then, to the great relief of all Israelites, "the Syrian raiding parties stopped invading the land of Israel" (2 Kings 6:23, author's translation).

---

1. The Hebrew word used here is *śāṭān*, "a satan," which in this verse refers to an earthly adversary or enemy. In other Old Testament verses it refers to Satan, the accuser who originated in heaven.

2. The Hebrew word for Naaman's disease has been translated "leprous, leper, leprosy" in English Bibles. Recent translations suggest in footnotes that it is probably not what is known today as leprosy, or Hansen's disease, but a less serious skin disease.

3. For an idea of the limits placed upon Naaman because of his disease, at least as it would have been in ancient Israel, see Leviticus 13:43–46 and Numbers 5:1–3.

4. The Hebrew expression *lipney,* "toward the faces," means to be in the presence of someone.

5. Quoted in Jyremy Reid and Tim Allston, "Black: God 'Texting Me' Gave Shutdown Prayers," *Adventist Review,* December 17, 2013, http://www.adventistreview.org/church-news/god-texting-me-gave-shutdown-prayers,-barry-black-said.

6. The Hebrew word *hālak,* "walk," is used here, making clear that the means of Naaman's travel to the Jordan River should be by foot, not by chariot.

7. This was suggested by Duane L. Christensen in *The Anchor Bible Dictionary,* vol. 2 (New York: Doubleday, 1992), s.v. "Gehazi."

8. Gerhard von Rad, *God at Work in Israel* (Nashville: Abingdon, 1980), 54.

9. Some of these stories have been collected and summarized by Andrea Sterk in "Mission From Below: Captive Women and Conversion on the East Roman Frontiers," *Church History* 79 (2010): 1–39.

Jonah: A Reluctant but Successful Missionary

"Stand up and start walking!" Seven times this blunt command of the Lord echoed in the ears of Old Testament persons.[1] They include Moses, Balaam, Elijah, Jeremiah, residents of Samaria and Jerusalem, and twice to the prophet Jonah, whose mission misadventures make required reading in the history of mission. For Jonah, God's direction was clear—"Stand up and start walking to Nineveh!" (Jonah 1:2, paraphrase).

Mission in the Bible is of two types: either "come" or "go." "Come" is the main type of mission in the Old Testament. God intended that the nations come to Israel because of her highly visible state of blessing by God. While there, the nations would witness Israel's worship of the true God, learn of His laws for healthy people living in a healthy society, and seek to make Israel's God theirs as well.

"Go" mission sends missionaries individually or in small groups out to the nations. Missionaries take the initiative in reaching people where they live. The Old Testament mentions a few "go" missionaries, such as the Israelite servant girl, Daniel, and Queen Esther. But their relocation among other nations was because of war, not part of a conscious mission strategy devised back home.

Jonah, however, is an exception. God's command for him to "go" breaks the Old Testament pattern of "come" mission. His story is a puzzle for those who make a special study of mission.[2] His experience is the topic of this week's lesson.

Background and personality

The Bible gives a few bare facts about Jonah. His father's name, his home village (Gath Hepher, located in Galilee between what later became the villages of Nazareth and Cana), and his calling as prophet are stated in 2 Kings 14:25. He told the ship's crew during the storm at sea, "I am Hebrew; I am in fear of Yahweh God of the heavens, who made the sea and the dry land" (Jonah 1:9, author's translation). He also told them that he was running away from Yahweh (verse 10). Best known about Jonah was his being swallowed by the "huge fish" (Jonah 2:1). His mission to Nineveh, when he finally got there, was successful. It freed that great city from evil and violence as its citizens called on God (Jonah 3:8).

But while bare facts are scarce, the Bible reveals more about the inner life and thought of this prophet-missionary than about any other biblical person except perhaps Jeremiah. Jonah's story uncovers the contrasts, conflicts, and oppositions of his inner life as they spilled over into his mission effort. Opposition and contrast are scattered throughout his story, both the internal ones and those in the outside situations in which he found himself. For example, even as Jonah stood on that pitching ship's deck, sailing west instead of walking east, his answer to the crew's questions included several opposites that would later become important: "Hebrew" (versus "Israelite"); "Yahweh, God of heaven" (versus the local god of Nineveh); "sea" versus "dry land" (Jonah 1:9).

Jonah, running *from* God

When God said, "Stand up and start walking!" Jonah "stood up" (verse 3), but not to walk to Nineveh. He stood up to "run away" from God. In human behavior Jonah's response is known as oppositional—doing the opposite of what one is asked. The road to Nineveh went first north and then east. The sea route to Tarshish went first south and then west—as far west as ships sailed in Jonah's day.

"He went down to Joppa." When the Hebrew Bible states that a person "went down," it might carry more meaning than just that they walked downhill. It can point to spiritual failure that grows out of an unwillingness to conform to the will of God, and it usually leads to difficulties. This was true for Abraham "going down" to Egypt (Genesis 12:10), Moses from Mount Sinai to the golden calf scenario (Exodus 32:15), Samson to Philistine territory (Judges 14:1), Saul to Gilgal (1 Samuel 15:12), and David to the wilderness of Paran (1 Samuel 25:1).

It was certainly true for Jonah. The phrase "he went down" is used four times to describe his four "goings-down" that were parts of his attempt to avoid Nineveh. First, Jonah "went down" (Jonah 1:3) from his village in the highlands of Galilee to the Mediterranean port city of Joppa, where he found a ship sailing westward. Next he "went down" into the ship's passenger quarters. As the storm tossed the ship, he "went down" into the hold, the lowest part of the ship. Jonah "went down" a fourth and final time when the great fish with him inside "went down" to "the roots of the mountains" (Jonah 2:6). No other person in the Hebrew Bible experienced such a four-stage "going down" as a result of spiritual rebellion.

In spite of his rebellion, however, God worked and waited as He prepared His chosen missionary for this mission.

Fares and excess baggage

Jonah's "paying the fare" is the only case in the Old Testament where money is connected with mission service. It is one of the three *m*'s of mission (message, manpower, money). Whose money did Jonah use to pay his fare? The story does not answer this question, but it raises an important point. Most donations for mission come from people with modest income. Mission money, therefore, needs to be used carefully.

Jonah's four "goings-down" robbed him of initiative. From the moment the crew found and woke him, he was completely passive, and God took over the situation. The windstorm had come from Him (Jonah 1:6). The crew, in desperation, dragged baggage onto the deck and threw it overboard. While doing that, they found Jonah curled up in a stupor.[3] He was uncaring and unengaged in their life-threatening situation, of no more use than the baggage around him (verse 5).

The crew then cast lots to identify the person responsible for the raging storm, and the lot pointed out Jonah. Jonah's lack of sympathy for the at-risk crew and passengers showed up at this point. He knew that they faced death because of him and that he was the cause of the storm. He knew also what he needed to do to save them: throw himself into the sea.

But he was too passive to jump overboard, asking instead that the crew throw him (verse 12). In their abhorrence of such an act, they tried in vain to save themselves. Finally, desperate, they followed God's instructions through Jonah; they picked him up and threw him overboard, like excess baggage (verse 15). Even in Jonah's passive, rebellion-induced stupor and his sense of ethnic superiority, God was not finished with him.

Jonah praying and running *to* God

The captain ordered Jonah to pray to his God for their lives (verse 6). But the only prayer aboard the ship was offered by the crew (verse 14). "Jonah prayed to the LORD his God" (Jonah 2:2) only after he was in the belly of the great fish. Jonah's prayer was self-centered, with no mention of the passengers and crew. The only reference to them in his prayer was a criticism of "those who cling to worthless idols" (verse 8). He could not know that, after they prayed and threw him overboard, "the raging sea grew calm" (Jonah 1:15) and that they then "offered a sacrifice to the LORD and made vows to him" (verse 16). They were saved because Jonah's God loved them, *not* because Jonah loved and prayed for them.

By the time Jonah's prayer was finished, he had learned to rejoice "with shouts of grateful praise" (Jonah 2:9). He also made up his mind to keep a vow he had once made to God. Through Jonah's brush with death, God had given him a new understanding of the importance of carrying out what he had promised: "What I have vowed I will make good" (verse 9).

Jonah: A Reluctant but Successful Missionary

This mention of an unkept vow gives the reader new insight into God's determination with Jonah. God kept His promises, and He expected His chosen people to keep theirs. Jonah also learned more about the last line of his prayer: "Salvation comes from the LORD." By this time he had experienced salvation three times: from shipwreck, from drowning, and from being digested.

With vomit[4] washed off and seaweed out of his hair, Jonah heard God's instruction a second time: "Stand up and start walking to Nineveh." This time he obeyed. During that inland journey of more than four hundred miles (640 kilometers), Jonah mixed with peoples with different religions and cultures than his own. Each step took him farther from his home in Gath Hepher and from the temple in Jerusalem, headquarters for the worship of his God. Every step also exposed him to further "contamination" by these heathen, which would have been very unsettling.

Jonah's experience of salvation at sea taught him what had been only theoretical theology earlier—that the Lord God of Israel was the One "who made the sea and the dry land" (Jonah 1:9). His Lord's jurisdiction truly extended out to sea. He had led Jonah through the sea in safety. Would He now do the same across those miles of dry land, with its foreigners, idols, false religions, nonkosher food, greedy innkeepers, wild animals, and highway bandits? Did the Lord's power really extend over all that land? Would it be effective in cosmopolitan Nineveh, "that great city" with its own powerful gods? And why was the Lord, whose earthly home was in Jerusalem, so interested in Assyrian Nineveh, Israel's enemy?

Jonah's every step raised another question. What did God want him to proclaim in Nineveh? "Preach against it," the Lord told him the first time (verse 2). "Proclaim to it the message I give you" was all that the Lord would tell him the second time (Jonah 3:2). The sins of Nineveh were spelled out with only two Hebrew words.

The first, *rā'āh,* is a general word best translated "evil, wickedness" but also "disaster, calamity, suffering." It occurs seven times in Jonah, providing a theme that appears in each major part of the book. It describes the condition of Nineveh and its inhabitants (Jonah 1:2; 3:8,

10), the storm at sea (verses 7, 8), and Jonah's personal upsets: a "great wrong" when the Lord changed His mind and did not destroy Nineveh (Jonah 4:1), and finally when the plant shading him relieved him of his "suffering" caused by the sunlight (verse 6).

The second Hebrew word describing the condition of Nineveh, *ḥāmās,* was part of the king's own testimony about the condition of the city: "Let them give up their evil ways and their *violence*" (Jonah 3:8). There is nothing vague or general about the meaning of *ḥāmās.* It first appears in God's description of the world's inhabitants in days just before the flood: "full of *violence*" (Genesis 6:11, 13). How much of Nineveh's evil, disaster, and violence would God ask Jonah to proclaim?

Jonah running *with* God

God gave Jonah details of his "gospel" before he reached Nineveh: "Forty more days and Nineveh will be overthrown" (Jonah 3:4). God had judged the city and found it wanting. Jonah was able to declare God's blunt message, just five Hebrew words, in a language the Ninevites understood. It certainly addressed their situation. They got the point. The "gospel" woke them up to their dire situation and awakened a need for survival. It appealed to every socioeconomic level, "from the greatest to the least" (verse 5). Their response was immediate— they "believed God" (verse 5).

From then on, the Ninevites and their king took over from Jonah. They called for fasting, sackcloth and ashes, prayer ("call urgently on God"), and giving up evil and violence (verse 8). Finally, the king called for hope—hope for the grace of God: "Who knows? God may yet relent . . . so that we will not perish" (verse 9). Jonah's proclamation of the "gospel" spelled out only the judgment, not deliverance, but the king saw the chance to be saved from destruction. God's warnings of judgment contained the offer of rescue for those willing to repent. "When God saw what they did and how they turned from their evil ways, he relented and did not bring on them the destruction he had threatened" (verse 10). This should have been the climax of the story. The Ninevites, their king, and Jonah could have "lived happily ever after." Apparently the Ninevites did, but not Jonah. His story continued.

Complaining Jonah running *ahead of* God

"But to Jonah this seemed very wrong, and he became angry." This is clear from his prayer, which can be paraphrased, "I knew this would happen! I clearly understood Your character, God, that You are gracious, merciful, slow to get angry, very loving, and You change Your mind about what You threaten! This is why I ran in the opposite direction!" (Jonah 4:2). Jonah then quotes God's own declaration about His character: "Merciful, gracious, longsuffering, loving, changing your mind about punishing evil people with disaster" (verse 2, paraphrase).[5]

This is the key description of Himself God declared to Moses during the golden calf incident, when God planned to destroy those worshiping the idol at the foot of Mount Sinai (Exodus 32–34). Moses pleaded for God to spare them, and God "changed His mind" (Exodus 32:14, NASB), just as He had now "changed His mind" and spared the Ninevites. Jonah's very existence, and that of his fellow Hebrews, depended on God changing His mind. Did Jonah remember that part of the Exodus story?

Nature lessons

After Jonah's angry prayer and appeal for death, God communicated in a more suitable way to get His message past Jonah's defenses. He used object lessons from nature. The expression "God appointed" (ESV) occurs three times to introduce the three natural things God used to awaken a sense of empathy in Jonah.

First, He "appointed" a castor bean plant that grew up overnight; the next morning it shaded Jonah's head in order literally "to deliver him from misery" (Jonah 4:6, author's translation). The following day at break of dawn God "appointed" a caterpillar that attacked the plant so that it withered (verse 7). Then at sunrise he "appointed" a scorching east wind that, along with the blazing sun, nearly caused Jonah to faint (verse 8). Jonah's journey, beginning in the watery deep of the sea, nearly ended on the roasting dry ground outside Nineveh's walls. Through these extremes of the natural environment God labored to implant a single lesson in this cold-hearted missionary—God loves all humans and empathizes with them in their suffering. He also loves the animals and wanted them spared from pointless slaughter. God needed Jonah to enlarge his empathy ability: "You mourn the loss of a single castor bean plant; shouldn't I pity those 120,000 Ninevites, and their herd animals?" (see verses 10, 11).

At the final reported sighting of Jonah, prophet and missionary, he was still in his humble twig hut under the withered castor bean plant. Did his prophecy about the restoration of Israel's borders follow his Nineveh experience (see 2 Kings 14:25)? We are not told. There is perhaps a passing reference to him in the work of his fellow prophet Hosea, who lived at the same time and ministered in the same area. Was Hosea making a sideways reference to Jonah when he prophesied the return of Israelites from a future captivity in Assyria: "They will come . . . from Assyria, fluttering like doves [Jonah, Hebrew, *yônah*]. I will settle them in their homes" (Hosea 11:11). Was Hosea making a passing reference to Jonah's return to Israel from Nineveh?

Jonah makes an appearance in the words of Jesus. When Jesus was casting out a demon, some onlookers called out for a sign from heaven to confirm His true identity (Luke 11:16). Jesus replied that an evil generation like theirs would be given only one sign, the sign of Jonah. He was a sign to the Ninevites that God meant what He said—they were on the inside track to destruction, and only repentance and giving up their evil would spare their city (Jonah 11:30). Those same Ninevites, in the final judgment, will stand up and condemn those who were given but rejected even greater light—the light brought by Jesus Himself (verse 32).

Conclusion

Jonah may have been a troubled missionary, but he pioneered what would become God's preferred method of future mission. God's work through him saved a great city and provided Jesus with a powerful object lesson for His own people in His day.

As the first called and commissioned "go" missionary, Jonah made mistakes. But these mistakes must be judged in light of his mission's astounding success. His personal theology needed to expand in order to take in this new mission method. It also needed to adjust to the surprising discovery of God's interest in the salvation of a faraway, rebellious people who posed a threat to the peace and security of Israel. Jonah's story has left following generations of children a wonderful story of the big fish and an astounding story of missionary (mis)adventure followed by success. Finally, Jonah's story shows how God's work of mission will not be stopped by the fallen humanity of His chosen mission agents.

---

1. Deuteronomy 10:22; Numbers 22:20; 1 Kings 17:9; Jeremiah 13:6; Micah 2:10; Jonah 1:2; 3:2.

2. See, for example, Arthur Glasser, *Announcing the Kingdom* (Grand Rapids, MI: Baker Academic, 2003), 64.

3. Hebrew *rādam* refers to Jonah's state: either very deeply asleep, or in a daze, stunned, knocked out.

4. Hebrew *qy'* "to vomit" (Jonah 2:11) occurs twelve times in the Hebrew Bible, a gustatory expression for the act of getting out of the system something objectionable.

5. This core description of the God of Israel, spoken by God Himself in Exodus 34:6, is repeated several places: Numbers 14:18; Psalms 86:15; 103:8; 145:8; Nahum 1:3; Nehemiah 9:17.

Daniel: Statesman, Prophet, Missionary

The stories in Daniel are some of the best known in the Bible. They have been reshaped and retold, especially for children. But the act of simplifying them has brought about losses for adults, because the stories in the first six chapters of Daniel also contain "adult themes" that are usually left off when told to and for children. A few of them, relevant for Daniel as missionary, are included in this chapter. While the visions in the second half of Daniel remain important for Adventists, the lessons about mission in the first half are also vital and will be the main focus of this week's lesson.

Faithful and promising young Israelite exile

Where were you when you came of age, crossing the line drawn by your culture that separates youth from adulthood? Were you in the familiar, warm embrace of a stable society, the one in which you lived your childhood, surrounded with family and familiar routines? Did you come of age while on the move between communities, due to a change of one parent's employment, or due to family breakdown, or as a civil war refugee? Did you come of age in an alien culture, where you spoke the minority language, had the minority appearance, and lived in a minority community? Were you emotionally on guard against the stares of the majority culture? Or were you "invisible" to the eyes of that culture? Did you have to watch your step to avoid becoming a target of emotional or even physical aggression due to your minority status?

Daniel and his companions experienced most of these scenarios as they came of age. Their first years were spent in upper-class Jerusalem homes. According to Daniel 1:4, they were among the royalty and aristocracy of Jerusalem. They were probably in their early teens when taken captive and exiled.[1] By the time Daniel interpreted Nebuchadnezzar's dream, they had reached the stage of life designated by the Aramaic word usually translated "man," because Daniel was introduced to the king with the words, "I have found among the Judean exiles a *man*" (Daniel 2:25, author's translation).[2]

Daniel and friends in Babylon

Daniel and companions completed a three-year course of study at the University of Babylon, on Nebuchadnezzar's orders, so that they could master "the language and literature of the Chaldeans" (verse 4, NKJV). Babylonian literature and science was among the most advanced in the ancient world. Daniel and his companions were at the very top of their graduating class, so impressing Nebuchadnezzar that he assigned them, straight out of school, to high positions in the Babylonian civil service (verses 17–20).

New languages such as Aramaic, Akkadian and Sumerian, Persian, and even some Egyptian confronted Daniel and his companions in their study and work. In order to please Nebuchadnezzar and serve his empire, they had to apply themselves to learn the languages. They probably also faced pressure to attend and perhaps offer Sabbath lectures. They would also have to read literature about the pagan gods that challenged their beliefs and values.

Homesickness often strikes, especially on one's first time away from home. Homesickness certainly strikes missionaries, and it struck Daniel and his companions. Homesickness crops up in Scripture, where we find a psalm about it:

By the rivers of Babylon we sat and wept
   when we remembered Zion.
There on the poplars
   we hung our harps,
for there our captors asked us for songs,
   our tormentors demanded songs of joy;
     They said, "Sing us one of the songs of Zion!"
How can we sing the songs of the Lord
   while in a foreign land? (Psalm 137:1–4).[3]

With just a touch of imagination one can see Daniel, Hananiah, Mishael, and Azariah in a group of captive University of Babylon students, on an outing to the Euphrates River just outside the city wall, speaking their native Hebrew language, singing this psalm to strumming harps, maybe shedding tears for their faraway families and former lives. Back at the university they were probably pressured to join their fellow students and attend required worship services at the moon god Sin's grand temple in downtown Babylon. These and many similar cultural, ethical, and religious confrontations would have complicated their lives in Babylon.

Food and drink

While Daniel and his fellow Hebrew students could sing psalms on their riverbank outings, back in Nebuchadnezzar's palace they had to face a different kind of "music"—the royal foods that King Nebuchadnezzar ordered for their dinner table. The food test was about more than just eating and drinking. It was about loyalty to God. "The king appointed for them a daily ration from the king's choice food and from the wine which he drank" (verse 5, NASB). The king wanted to nourish his handpicked university students, to accustom them to the high life of court. So he ordered that they eat the same "choice food" that he ate.[4]

Surviving recipes and menus from Babylon and nearby countries give an idea of that "choice food." Refined flour would have set royal food apart from food of ordinary citizens, according to an ancient Sumerian proverb: "Fine flour is appropriate for women and the palace."[5] A cake recipe for the palace in the Chaldean city of Ur is rich even by today's standards. It included butter, white cheese, first-quality dates, and raisins.[6] Meat appeared on royal tables far more often than on ordinary ones, as indicated by the following ancient inscription: "Let the gods eat roasted meat, roasted meat, roasted meat. . . . After preparing a serving platter made of gold, place on it pieces of roasted meat."[7] After being presented to the gods at their temple, the untouched "leftovers" would have been rushed to Nebuchadnezzar's palace tables. Grilled locusts, anyone?

But Daniel and companions had a different idea of "choice food." Their ideal menu did not match Nebuchadnezzar's. Theirs was much older, originating at Creation. Diet was so important, even in the pre-fall world, that the Creator's "menu" appears twice in the Creation story, in Genesis 1:29 and again in 2:16, 17.[8] Having people eat right was important for the Creator, and so it was important for Daniel and his companions. They refused to eat the king's fare, choosing instead a diet closer to what they knew was God's will. We know, too, from Daniel 2 how well their faithfulness was rewarded.

Scripture informs us that there was another royal Hebrew captive living in Babylon in Daniel's day—the Judean king Jehoiachin. His eating practice is also recorded: "Jehoiachin . . . for the rest of his life ate regularly at the king's table" (2 Kings 25:29).[9] This lack of consistency, one Hebrew eating royal food while another refused it, must have complicated the lives of Daniel and his companions. Even as captives, they were missionaries, standing for principle. Even without words, whenever they ate a meal they were already missionaries.

Serving King Nebuchadnezzar

How did Daniel, as a high-ranking government official, keep his office, or even his head, during a nearly seventy-year career (Daniel 1:21) in the face of scheming rivals and major changes of rulers? He was the target of two royal death decrees (Daniel 2:5–13; 6:6–9) and was saved by God's direct action in the lions' den (Daniel 6:10–22), as were his companions in the furnace (Daniel 3:19–27). The answer may be found in the passing mention of some of Daniel's character traits, which are scattered through the book. They include excellence, integrity, visible loyalty to God, willingness to serve, active prayer life, and the ability to speak diplomatically and wisely.

The excellence of Daniel and companions appears in the following passages: "As for these four young men God gave knowledge and understanding of all kinds of literature and learning. And Daniel could understand visions and dreams of all kinds" (Daniel 1:17). "In every matter of wisdom and understanding about which the king questioned them, he found them ten times better than all the magicians and enchanters in his whole kingdom" (verse 20). "There is a man in your kingdom who has the spirit of the holy gods in him. In the time of your father he was found to have insight and intelligence and wisdom like that of the gods . . . This man Daniel, whom the king called Belteshazzar, was found to have a keen mind and knowledge and understanding, and also the ability to interpret dreams, explain riddles and solve difficult problems" (Daniel 5:11, 12). "Now Daniel so distinguished himself among the administrators and the satraps by his exceptional qualities" (Daniel 6:3). "You who are highly esteemed" (Daniel 10:11, 19).

Daniel's integrity appears in the first chapter: "Daniel resolved not to defile himself with the royal food and wine, and he asked the chief official for permission not to defile himself in this way" (Daniel 1:8). "Keep your gifts for yourself, and give your rewards to someone else" (Daniel 5:17). "They could find no corruption in him, because he was trustworthy and neither corrupt nor negligent" (Daniel 6:4). "We will never find any basis for charges against this man Daniel" (verse 5).

Daniel's loyalty to God was clear to anyone who was close enough to watch: "Now when Daniel learned that the decree had been published, he went home to his upstairs room where the windows opened towards Jerusalem. Three times a day he got down on his knees and prayed, giving thanks to his God, just as he had done before. Then these men . . . found Daniel praying" (verses 10, 11). "May your God, whom you serve continually" (verse 16). "Has your God, whom you serve continually" (verse 20). "When Daniel was lifted from the den, no wound was found on him, because he had trusted in his God" (verse 23). The power of even wordless example helped the missionary Daniel testify to God's goodness.

Daniel was not afraid to serve. He and his companions showed an attitude of service to the king and country of Babylon, despite what had been done to their city and families. "I, Daniel, was exhausted and lay ill for several days. Then I got up and went about the king's business" (Daniel 8:27). "How can I, your servant, talk with you, my lord?" (Daniel 10:17). Daniel could have spent his adult life angry and resentful because of his Babylonian captivity. But God helped him rise above those feelings and serve his God and his people.

Prayer was real for Daniel and his companions: "[Daniel] urged [Hananiah, Mishael, and Azariah] to plead for mercy from the God of heaven. . . . Then Daniel praised the God of heaven" (Daniel 2:18, 19). "Three times a day he got down on his knees and prayed, giving thanks to his God, just as he had done before" (Daniel 6:10). "I turned to the LORD God and pleaded with him in prayer and petition, in fasting, and in sackcloth and ashes. I prayed to the LORD my God and confessed" (Daniel 9:3, 4). The following fifteen verses record one of the longest prayers in Scripture. Daniel's prayers got answers: "Since the first day that you set your mind to gain understanding and to humble yourself before your God, your words were heard, and I have come in response to them" (Daniel 10:12).

In Daniel's highly visible, public role, he had to speak as the diplomat that God wanted him to be. "Then Daniel spoke to him *with wisdom and tact*" (Daniel 2:14; emphasis added). "As for me, this mystery has been revealed to me, *not because I have greater wisdom than other living men*" (verse 30; emphasis added). "My lord, if only the dream applied to your enemies and its meaning to your adversaries!" (Daniel 4:19). "May the king, live forever!" (Daniel 6:21).These samples of Daniel's diplomatic speaking skills help the reader understand how careful he was with words. He respected the formal manner of address in use at the royal courts where he served. At the same time, he spoke honestly, humbly, and truthfully

Daniel, the nations, and the future

Daniel's special skill of interpreting the visions and dreams of others (see Daniel 1:17) proved very useful for him in his other major role:

receiving and interpreting visions and dreams about God's plan for the nations. Had Daniel remained in Jerusalem, he would have lacked the firsthand experience of the fact that God indeed rules over nations and peoples well beyond Israel's borders. He would not have been so well qualified to receive and write out the most significant visions of the future to be found in the Hebrew Bible.

Daniel's visions became an important foundation for Jesus' later teaching about the kingdom of God, its people, and their relationship to the nations. Daniel's vision in chapter 7 provided the important "Son of man" title that Jesus used, and it outlined the sequence of the four earthly empires that would become absorbed into the future everlasting kingdom that God will establish.

The doctrine of the second coming of Christ is strongly supported by Daniel's visions. The clearest Hebrew Bible statement of the doctrine of the general resurrection of the dead, both the righteous and the unrighteous, at the end of time, is in Daniel (12:2). The "good news" that God's people will endure a great time of tribulation just before the end is part of Daniel's message for the future (12:1).

During his long stay in Babylon and Persia, Daniel laid a sound foundation for the future of his people who remained there. Many never returned to Jerusalem at the end of the Babylonian exile, choosing instead to remain in Babylon. Daniel himself spent the rest of his life in Babylon and Persia, where he eventually died and was buried in the Persian city of Susa (also spelled Shusan). He was the ideal model of a long-term "missionary" who adapted without compromising his principles and who served with excellence—without absorbing the pagan values that surrounded him. His example of non-compromise on faith essentials, excellence in service, and diligence in adapting to his adoptive culture helped prepare that region to receive with some tolerance and goodwill the Jewish exiles and their children who chose to stay.

Conclusion: Daniel and God's last-day people

Daniel lived through the catastrophic fall of Jerusalem. About sixty-five years later he lived through the fall of Babylon. He adapted to the culture of the Babylonian and Persian courts, but without compromising biblical standards. He used his faith, prayer life, insight into dreams and visions, and diplomacy skills, along with his pagan education, in the service of foreign powers. His silent and spoken testimony resulted in empire-wide royal decrees declaring the reality of his God and commanding His worship.

Through vision, Daniel experienced the coming of the Son of man and the fall of last-day Babylon. But God told him that quite a lot of time would pass between his day and those events. He himself would not live through the final time of trouble. "As for you, go your way till the end. You will rest, and then at the end of the days you will rise to receive your allotted inheritance" (Daniel 12:13).

What a surprise awaits Daniel on the day of resurrection, when he sees for himself the enormous, worldwide stretch of the kingdom of God, including people from "every nation, tribe, language and people" (Revelation 14:6), whom he saw in those visions while an involuntary missionary in Babylon and Persia so long ago.

---

1. Hebrew *yeled,* "boy, young adolescent," occurs five times in Daniel chapter 1.

2. Aramaic *gĕbar,* "man, adult male," is used in Daniel 2:25 and nine additional times, referring to Daniel and/or his three companions.

3. Jamaican musicians Brent Dowe and Trevor McNaughton wove these verses of Psalm 137 into a popular song in 1970 titled "Rivers of Babylon." The 1978 recording by the Caribbean vocalists in Boney M. became a worldwide hit.

4. The word *pathbag,* translated in the NASB "choice food," is Old Persian. It occurs in Daniel 1:5 and five more times in Daniel.

5. Cathy K. Kaufman, *Cooking in Ancient Civilizations* (Westport, CT: Greenwood Press, 2006), 11.

6. Ibid., 32, 33.

7. This is part of a text cut into the wall of a temple in Uruk. Jean Bottéro, *The Oldest Cuisine in the World: Cooking in Mesopotamia* (Chicago: University of Chicago Press, 2004), 43.

8. In these verses, a total of forty Hebrew words were devoted to communicating the Creator's food instructions. This is more than 5 percent of the total number of words in the Creation account of Genesis chapters 1 and 2.

9. Judean king Jehoiachin is named in a clay tablet listing the amounts of olive oil to be supplied to his household in exile by the royal kitchen in Babylon. The kitchen also supplied the other items that made up a Babylonian royal diet. See http://www.biblearchaeology.org /post/2008/04/28/Nebo-Sarsekim-Found-in-Babylonian-Tablet.aspx#Article.

CHAPTER 6

Esther and Mordecai: Rescuers of the Jewish People

Esther was born about thirty years too late to have met Daniel, even though both lived in the Persian city of Shushan. But she probably visited his tomb there. Let us assume for a moment that on a visit to Daniel's tomb, Esther started an imaginary conversation with him on their experiences as exiles who were swept suddenly as "missionaries" of sorts into the royal court of the region's superpower. In this imaginary conversation, Esther and Daniel would share their mission vision. Both were on a mission to a hostile royal court. Danger was always present.

Esther reached adulthood at a time when Persian society was undergoing social unrest over the question of women's and men's roles. It was at such a time that God placed her in a highly visible position and kept her Jewishness secret in order to carry out a risky mission to save the Jewish people living in Persia.

Orphan Esther becomes queen of Persia

Esther was the orphaned daughter of Abihail. Like all girls and unmarried women in that culture who were without fathers, she was under the authority of her nearest male relative, her cousin Mordecai, who made sure she was safe and cared for until she married. As a young woman, Esther came to the attention of the king's agents looking for suitable entries for the royal beauty contest. She had "a lovely figure and was beautiful" (Esther 2:7). Could her beauty be considered a spiritual gift? The Hebrew expression translated "lovely figure" is used to describe the figures of only three biblical women: Rachel, for whose bride price Jacob labored fourteen years; Abigail, who stopped an angry David in his tracks by prostrating herself at his feet; and Esther, who would prostrate herself at the king's feet at a crucial stage of her mission (Esther 8:3).[1]

Esther's culture did not empower her to refuse to enter the royal beauty contest. Like other young women of that culture, she lacked that right, as is clear from the wording of the passage: "Many young women *were brought*. . . . Esther also *was taken*" (Esther 2:8, emphasis added). Her role at that time was to be an object of sexual appeal. When she was selected to appear in the beauty contest, her guardian Mordecai "commanded" Esther not to disclose her people and tribe (verse 10, ESV). This probably meant she could not request special food as Daniel had done; that would give away her Jewishness. In order to keep secret her Jewishness (verses 8–12), she would have to eat whatever the palace kitchen put on her plate during her full year of preparation.

A full year of beauty preparation was required (verse 12). In addition to the oils, cleansings, and perfumes mentioned, the preparation would include coaching in the customs, manners, and rituals expected of royalty. There would have been special stress put on the wifely submission that a future queen would demonstrate as a role model to wives across the empire. This seems highly unusual training for a future missionary, but the Lord worked through those oils and perfumes, turning them into powerful "anointings" of Esther as He prepared her for her unusual mission, the next step of which was a night with the king (verse 14).

Did Esther commit a sin by spending the night with Ahasuerus? The Bible does not comment on the morality of that event. Nor does it state that they slept together, although readers can assume they did. The passage does state that each beauty contestant, after her night with the king, went to "the second house of the women," which was supervised by "the king's eunuch who was in charge of the concubines" (verse 14). In other words, Esther became a concubine.

Hebrew law did not recognize concubines, but they were part of the day-to-day reality in Israel. Patriarchs Abraham and Jacob had concubines, as did Caleb and Gideon. Concubines were especially a feature of kingship: Saul, David, Solomon, and Rehoboam, and probably most other kings of Israel and Judah, had concubines, contrary to the command in Deuteronomy 17:17. It is also important to remember that Esther had little authority over her own life and person.

Esther came into her role as queen at a time when a royal order was in force on married women across the empire to submit to their husbands (Esther 1:22). As first lady of the empire, she was expected to be a role model for women across Persia of wifely submission to her husband.

Culture conflict in Esther's training for mission

How far should missionaries adapt to the culture in which they serve? Can Esther's unusual experience help answer this question for today's missionaries-in-training? While her childhood religious upbringing had prepared her for adult life as a faithful Jew in exile, her special mission called for extra training and support. Palace staff did their part of the yearlong preparation for the beauty contest. The royal eunuch Hegai, who looked after the king's women, quickly supplied what Esther needed for her year of beautification (Esther 2:9) and gave her inside information to increase her chance of winning the king's favor (verse 15).

God worked through Mordecai, Esther's cousin and adoptive parent, to prepare her. Mordecai was determined from the moment the beauty contest was announced that Esther would have a role in protecting the Jews. His support of Esther had three stages. The first started at her birth as his cousin into their extended family. The second began when she was orphaned and Mordecai adopted her. The third began as she was taken from Mordecai's home in Shushan and put into the palace along with the other young women for the year of intense training.

Esther responded to Mordecai's support with loyal obedience. Even as queen, Esther continued to obey Mordecai. When royal permission for the planned genocide of the Jews was announced, Mordecai "instruct[ed] her to go into the king's presence to beg for mercy and plead with him for her people" (Esther 4:8).

Finally, the entire Jewish community of exiles in Shushan supported Esther as she prepared for the crucial moment of her mission, and of her life—an uninvited appearance before the king. This time *she* gave an order, which Mordecai obeyed: to call on the Jews in Shushan to join her and her maidens for three days of fasting and prayer to support her as she made an uninvited appearance before the king, hoping to awaken royal attention and sympathy, and not royal rage.

Living and witnessing during social change

The opening chapter of the book of Esther informs the reader of social change across the Persian Empire, focusing on the relationship between wives and husbands.[2] Queen Vashti[3] was expected to be a passive object of beauty, groomed to capture attention, and then direct it beyond herself to the king. She was an ornament at the king's side, attracting public admiration for him. But when the king asked her to leave her own banquet for the women of Shushan and come with her turban[4] to display her beauty before the men at their banquet, she refused.[5] This was no minor marital disagreement behind closed doors. It was public and highly visible. Something had to be done.

King and advisors responded with an empire-wide campaign to keep wives submissive and husbands assertive. The king issued a decree with three requirements. First, women were to give honor to the male head of household. Second, men were to take charge at home: "every man should be ruler over his own household" (Esther 1:22). Third, men were to use the language of their household. (The meaning of this part is not clear, but its lesson for modern missionaries is to learn and use the language of the people among whom they live and work.) The decree indicated that the roles of both husbands and wives were under stress from social change. Some feared that if wives did not submit to their husbands in all matters, they would weaken the social fabric of the empire.

Esther and Mordecai: Rescuers of the Jewish People

It was a challenging time to be king, and especially to be queen.

Haman plots genocide

Royal officer Haman decided to use the wife-husband social unrest across Persia as a cover for getting rid of an ethnic group he hated: the Jews. Like Mordecai and Esther, Haman was on a mission. His was genocide. While the word *genocide* (the organized killing of a people group sharing a common culture or ethnicity) was coined as recently as 1944,[6] the practice is ancient. The only reason stated in the Bible for Haman's grudge against the Jews, and especially against Mordecai, was his rage against Mordecai, who would not bow to him (Esther 3:5).

The lives of Esther, Mordecai, and all other Jews in the empire were threatened. If Haman managed to carry out his plot, it would have not only destabilized the empire but also undermined God's planned role for the Jewish people to save the world. Something had to be done.

Esther intercedes for her people

Through Esther, God's plan to save His people and, at the same time, bring awareness of His chosen people to the empire took a big step forward. Mordecai pointed out to Esther the reality of the death facing her—whether she acted to save her people or not. If she was not killed for approaching the king without his approval, her Jewishness would become known during the genocide, and she too would be killed (Esther 4:13, 14).

Readers of Esther have puzzled over the fact that God is not named even once in the book, while King Ahasuerus is named thirty times, Haman fifty-four times, Esther fifty-five times, and Mordecai fifty-eight times. But God's influence shows itself over and over in the timing of important events. Like Daniel and his friends, Esther and Mordecai saw God's hand in the times and seasons that He set in His own wisdom. Things happened at the right moment. People were in the right place when the time was right. This happened for Esther and Mordecai too often to be explained in any other way than God's providence.

The king also understood the importance of knowing the right time for events in his work administering the empire. He had special advisors whose title was "wise men who understood the times" (Esther 1:13). But God's people had even better knowledge of the times than did the king's "wise men." Mordecai was in the right place and at the right time to learn of a plot to assassinate the king. He exposed the plot, thus saving the king's life (Esther 2:21–23). The king, during a sleepless night, listened to the reading of the royal records just in time to learn of Mordecai's role in stopping the assassination.

God arranged for Mordecai to be honored by Haman on the day that Haman intended to have Mordecai killed (Esther 5:12–6:13). God's timing was always exact—not too early, not too late. Esther needed to keep quiet about her Jewishness for a time, but Mordecai understood when her time of silence should end. God now needed her to speak for her people. Mordecai sent a message to inform her it was time to speak for her people. It has become a well-known Bible quotation: "Who knows but that you have come to royal position for such a time as this?" (Esther 4:14).

Esther's cooperation with God's timing now takes center stage. She called her people to three days of fasting and prayer. On the third day she dressed and groomed herself as only the beautiful and shapely Queen Esther could and then stood facing the king. What would he do? He held out the golden scepter, signaling his welcome! Once again God had helped her find "favor in his sight" (Esther 5:2, NKJV). Her sense of God's timing prevented her blurting out her fear to the king then and there. Instead, she invited him and Haman to the first of two banquets. Only at the right time, during the second banquet, did Esther reveal her Jewishness and plead at the king's feet for herself and her people. In the meantime, God timed yet other events. Before that day had ended, Haman's plan to kill Mordecai had been reversed and Haman was dead.

Triumph of the Jews over their enemies

But Mordecai and the rest of the Jews across the Persian Empire were still not safe. They were still under a royal decree of genocide. Perhaps they were praying David's prayer: "May all who want to take my life be put to shame and confusion; may all who desire my ruin be turned back in disgrace" (Psalm 40:14).

Could the death decree be canceled? It was now part of the law of the Persians, which could not be changed. It could be made ineffective only by issuing another decree to counter it. The decree specified that the genocide would take place on the thirteenth day of Adar, the twelfth month of that year. It was now late in Sivan, the third month. Was there time to replace that decree and to communicate it to the ends of the empire? The fastest communication at the time was limited to the speed of horses and camels. According to Esther 8:14, the replacement decree giving Jews the right of self-defense was placed in the hands of messengers who rode with the decree through the empire.

On the thirteenth day of Adar, in the twelfth year of the reign of King Ahasuerus, the genocide decree came into effect. The Jews, permitted by the second decree to defend themselves, stood against their enemies who attacked them (Esther 8:13; 9:1). They vigorously defended their persons and property across the empire. But they did not take the property of their defeated attackers, even though it was the custom of ancient warfare, and even though the king's second decree permitted them to take their attackers' property (Esther 8:11). This helped reduce social disturbance caused by the failed genocide.

There was a strange and unexpected consequence of the second decree and the Jewish celebrations that took place as word spread: "Many people of other nationalities became Jews because fear of the Jews had seized them" (verse 17). They must have seen that the Jews had divine favor working on their behalf and, thus, they wanted to be part of such a community.

Conclusion: Feast of Purim

Esther's public mission was not finished. Before disappearing back into the palace as queen, she issued one more official letter to the Jews of the empire, setting up the yearly Purim festival as a celebration of peace and security (Esther 9:29). Esther's final action is the issuing of a decree for Jews to celebrate the anniversary of the salvation of Persia's Jews. This festival became known as Purim (verses 29–32).

The rest of Esther's life is a closed book. Nothing else is known about her. Her strange preparation for her mission and its highly secret nature set her apart from the experience of most women missionaries, although the records of Christian mission include stories of some amazing women.

As for Mordecai, his role became even more public after the success of the mission. Like Daniel before him, Mordecai rose in rank to second in authority to the king in the administration of the empire. This made it possible for him to sustain his dual mission service: loyalty to his king and support of his fellow Jews.

---

1. This Hebrew expression is also used to describe the first group of cows coming out of the Nile River in Pharaoh's dream: "plump of flesh, and with a lovely figure" (Genesis 41:18, author's translation).

2. Twenty-one percent of the Hebrew words in the book of Esther, 233 out of 1099, are devoted to tensions within the husband-wife relationship in the story of Queen Vashti.

3. Vashti's name occurs ten times in the book of Esther. Its meaning is uncertain but possibly "desired."

4. While the Hebrew word can refer to a crown, in a Persian setting it most likely refers to a turban.

5. Because Esther 1:1 literally translates, "bring Vashti before the king with her royal turban," some interpreters understand that she was to wear only the turban before the king and his banquet guests. This understanding is possible, but the text does not state it.

6. See the *Oxford English Dictionary,* 2nd ed. (Oxford: Oxford University Press, 1989), s.v. "genocide."

CHAPTER 7

Jesus, Author and Master of Missions

Our study of mission in the Scriptures now carries us past the time period covered by the Hebrew Bible and brings us to the New Testament era. This big leap covers not only time but also culture and religious belief and practice. The world of the New Testament differs from that of the Old Testament. The commitment to mission by God—Father, Son, and Holy Spirit—is a constant through the entire Bible. However, approach and method undergo change in the move from the world of the Old Testament to that of the New.

This lesson is the first of two focusing on the role of Jesus in God's mission. In this week's lesson on Jesus as author of missions and master of mission, the following themes will be covered: Old Testament roots of the mission of Jesus; the deep cultural divide that made separate missions necessary for Jews and for Gentiles; and Jesus' commissioning of His disciples to continue the mission He started. The chapter will close with a look at Christian mission and its success as a sign of Christ's second coming.

Jesus' mission foretold in the Old Testament

As already noted in chapter 4, the type of mission that dominated

Old Testament thought was the "come" type, in which the nations would come to Israel to see and learn of God's wish to fulfill His will, spoken to Abraham, to bless all families of the earth. Jonah was the only Old Testament "go" missionary sent out to a foreign country. But Old Testament revelation presents God as Creator of the whole world and deeply committed to it. Even passages that focus on the Hebrew people can express God's involvement with the people of the entire world; for example, "the LORD, the God of the spirits of all flesh . . ." (Numbers 27:16, NASB).

Israel's need for an individual Savior was a theme taken up especially by the prophets, who used several figures to communicate this important stage of God's saving plan for Israel and the nations.

One is king. The word *king* occurs more than two thousand times in the Old Testament, nearly always referring to a king of Israel or one of the surrounding nations. One Israelite king, David, stood out as a model by which others were judged. David received a message from God through the prophet Nathan that, even though David himself would die, God would continue to bless his descendants and establish his family, kingdom, and throne for all future time (2 Samuel 7:16). Later Israelites clung tightly to this promise. Even when the king currently on the throne "did what was evil in the sight of the Lord," they looked forward to the time when the righteous descendant of David would reign and lead the Hebrew nation to the holy and righteous life God had promised. Note Zechariah 9:9:

> Rejoice greatly, Daughter Zion!
>   Shout, Daughter Jerusalem!
> See, your king comes to you,
>   righteous and victorious,
> lowly and riding on a donkey.

Against the background of this Old Testament hope, it is easy to understand the excitement of the Jerusalem crowd when Jesus made His triumphal entry on Palm Sunday, riding a donkey (Matthew 21:2–11).

It was through their prophets that Old Testament Israelites learned about the coming Savior. Prophecies describing Him used images that had meaning for people in their culture: King, Messiah,[1] Immanuel,[2] Servant of the Lord, Son of God, Son of man. The expected Messiah would bring salvation to the Jewish people and reunite them, ending their long spiritual exile among the nations.

Other Old Testament savior figures also pointed to Jesus. In His Sabbath sermon in Nazareth, Jesus applied the anointed Messiah of Isaiah 61:1 to Himself (Luke 4:16–21). The Son of man, according to Daniel 7:13, 14, was a being who would receive from God such authority and power that all nations would worship Him. He would set up a kingdom that would last forever, unlike the series of failing empires that appeared earlier in Daniel's vision. Jesus used the title to refer to Himself frequently, according to the Gospels. Other Old Testament figures include Immanuel, the Prince, Prince of Peace, Servant of the Lord, and Prophet.

When would this savior figure arrive to help Israel? Daniel provided the most detailed timing information in his vision of 9:24–27. Jesus arrived at the time prophesied by Daniel. How would His people and the nations respond?

Jesus: Destined for the nations from birth

With the story of the wise men, Matthew's Gospel prepares readers for the worldwide reach of the gospel: "Magi from the east came to Jerusalem and asked, 'Where is the one who has been born king of the Jews? We saw his star in the east and have come to worship him' " (Matthew 2:1, 2).

These Magi, Medo-Persian "wise men," were known across the ancient world as experts in understanding the signs of the times. They learned about important events by studying the stars. Before modern high-speed communication, the heavens provided the quickest means for alerting people about special events. God Himself designed this "instant" means of communication and built it into creation: "Let there be lights in the vault of the sky to separate the day from the night, *and let them serve as signs*" (Genesis 1:14; emphasis added).[3] When the

Magi reported to King Herod that they had seen the star of the new king of the Jews in the east (Matthew 2:2), they were carrying out one of their main jobs—watching for and interpreting the heavenly signs of special events. But they did something more; they were the first of many Gentiles who would be given a message about Jesus so they could search for and worship Him.

Luke's account of Jesus' birth openly proclaims that Jesus would work for the salvation of all people. Angels declared to the shepherds "good news that will cause great joy for all the people" (Luke 2:10). The wise old Simeon, who met the infant Jesus and His parents at the temple forty days after His birth, declared that Jesus would be the "salvation which you [God] have prepared in the sight of *all nations;* a light for revelation to the *Gentiles*" (verses 30–32; emphasis added). John the Baptist, whose ministry prepared the way for that of Jesus, used the words of Isaiah 40:5 in order to foretell Jesus' mission. In Him "*all people* will see God's salvation" (Luke 3:6; emphasis added).

John's Gospel does not include the story of Jesus' birth, but it quotes the words of John the Baptist, who, when he saw Jesus, declared Him to be "the Lamb of God, who takes away the sin of the world!" (John 1:29). The message is repeated in the Bible's best-known verse: "For God so loved *the world* that he gave his one and only Son, that whoever believes in him shall not perish but have eternal life" (John 3:16; emphasis added). By these and other expressions, the Gospels prepare readers to understand that the mission of Jesus would go beyond the Jewish people of His day to include the nations.

Jesus: Mission to Jews

Jesus carried forward His mission with a good sense of timing (see John 7:6, 8). He knew that the Jewish people had a role in God's mission, and He worked to establish a strong Jewish center and base for His mission. Each Gospel makes clear the Jewishness of Jesus; He was born and brought up in the heart of Judaism, immersed in all its key beliefs and practices.

Jesus also worked according to a plan. An important part of it was to get into correct balance the three basic parts of His mission strategy.

These appear in the words of Matthew 4:23—"*teaching* in their synagogues, *proclaiming* the good news of the kingdom, and *healing* every disease and sickness among the people" (emphasis added). The Gospels reported the huge success of His work as a result of this balancing. Each was important, and each supported the others. Mission plans should be regularly checked to see that they reflect a healthy balance of these three parts. Is one part neglected? Has Adventist mission sometimes neglected part two while moving ahead with parts one and three?

Jesus knew how important it was to be a strong center from which to launch mission. He understood God's plan called for Him to be that center, to which the Jewish people would come. What had God given the Jewish people to equip them to serve as the center for Jesus' mission? First and most important, they had God's Word, the Bible. Most Jewish homes could not afford the expense of a complete hand-copied Bible, so they attended synagogue every Sabbath, and often on other days, where the main activity was reading and explaining the Hebrew Bible, along with prayer.

Second, to refresh their faith in the Bible's message that they had been chosen and blessed by God, the Jews repeated a set of memorized verses twice every day. They opened with Deuteronomy 6:4, 5: "Hear O Israel, the LORD our God, the LORD is one. Love the LORD your God with all your heart and with all your soul and with all your strength."[4] This twice-daily prayer also called on each Jew to honor the commandments and instructions, which the one true God had given them in the Scriptures. These memorized verses reminded Jesus and His fellow Jews twice each day to stay faithful to the one true God. This was especially helpful for those living among people who believed in many gods, or no God at all.

Third, Jews were expected to memorize their statement of fundamental beliefs, which in Jesus' day were eighteen in number. They were also expected to recite them three times each day.[5] This statement affirmed God as Creator, stated the importance of His law, praised God's power over death, and named Him as the source of true knowledge and wisdom. Woven through these fundamental beliefs were repeated expressions of the Jewish hope for coming salvation through a Redeemer (beliefs 1 and 7), and most important for this week's lesson, for a coming Son of David who would bring salvation (belief 15). In other words, belief in and hope for the coming Jewish Savior were on the lips and in the hearts of Jewish people three times each day, whether they lived in Palestine or in one of the many diaspora communities scattered through the ancient world.

Jesus also worked patiently choosing and preparing His disciples to take up, and eventually take over, His mission. Ten of their names in Matthew 10:2–4 are clearly Hebrew. But two, Andrew and Philip, are Greek. They were probably from Greek-speaking Jewish families. They became connecting links between Greek-speaking Jews and Jesus (see John 12:21, 22). As part of their preparation for their first go-it-alone missions, Jesus instructed them, "Do not go among the Gentiles or enter any town of the Samaritans. Go rather to the lost sheep if Israel" (Matthew 10:5, 6).

Jesus: Mission to the Gentiles

Jesus made clear that His first mission was to the Jews. But because of the message of some Old Testament prophecies, people began to understand His mission would someday go well beyond His own people. Several prophecies stated that the Messiah's saving mission would stretch beyond the Jews to offer salvation to other people groups as well: "The people [Galilee of the Gentiles] walking in darkness have seen a great light; on those living in the land of the shadow of death a light has dawned" (Isaiah 9:2, quoted in Matthew 4:14–16). "A light for the Gentiles" (Isaiah 42:6 and 49:6, quoted in Luke 2:32 and Acts 13:47). "I will pour out my Spirit on all people" (Joel 2:28, quoted in Acts 2:17). "I will send some of those who survive to the nations. . . . They will proclaim my glory among the nations" (Isaiah 66:19, quoted in Acts 2:5–12). Each of these passages names and includes "Gentiles" (the word refers to non-Jewish people) or "all people" in God's plan for Israel's future. The Messiah was thus expected to operate a two-phase mission, first for Jews, later for Gentiles.

Luke, in his Gospel and the book of Acts, gives the clearest message that Jesus had a worldwide mission that would include all peoples. He started in the opening chapter of his Gospel. While Matthew traced Jesus' ancestors back to Abraham, patriarch of the Jewish people, Luke included twenty generations of pre-Hebrew ancestors, beginning with Adam (Luke 3:23–38). The point of Luke's list of Jesus' ancestors is clear—as descendant of Adam, Jesus came to offer salvation to all of Adam's descendants.

Some of Jesus' own acts and words pointed to a wider mission. He healed a few Gentiles who approached Him: the centurion's servant (Matthew 8:5–13), the demon-possessed man (Mark 5:1–20), and the Canaanite woman's daughter (Matthew 15:21–28). But it was in Jesus' parables that the coming mission to the world was made clear. Wednesday's page of this week's lesson lists parables pointing to a mission to the world. The following phrases from these parables would have helped communicate a worldwide mission: "the field is the world"; "who is my neighbor?"; "compel them to come in so my house can be full!"; "I will set out and go back to my father."

In private conversation with His disciples, Jesus tried to prepare them for the quick growth of mission in the Gentile world. When explaining the parable of the sower and the seed, He clearly stated that "the field is the world" (Matthew 13:38). Their memory of His explanation would help them understand and support the rapid cross-cultural spread of the gospel, which would soon carry most of them far from their Galilean homeland.

The Great Commission

The risen Christ, just before the end of His time on earth, gave His disciples their "marching orders" for their soon-to-begin role in taking the gospel to the world. It is important to recall the dramatic events those disciples had recently survived—the arrest, trial, crucifixion, death, and resurrection of Jesus. Their understanding of His person, His nature, and His role as Savior of the world had jumped ahead of where it had been. In what must have been His final meeting with them, Jesus first informed them of His new role: *"All authority in heaven and on earth has been given to me"* (Matthew 28:18, emphasis added). His disciples would recognize that He was quoting Daniel's vision of the Son of man: "In my vision at night I looked, and there before me was one like a son of man, coming with the clouds of heaven. He approached the Ancient of Days and was led into his presence. *He was given authority, glory and sovereign power*" (Daniel 7:13, 14; emphasis added).

Then Jesus stated the Great Commission. Note in the following very literal translation, the key action word of the command is italicized: "After having walked, *make disciples* (or *students*) of all the nations, [by] baptizing them . . . teaching them" (Matthew 28:18, 19). The language draws on ancient Jewish teacher-student relationships. The stress is clearly on teaching more than on baptizing. Both Jesus and Paul focused on teaching more than on baptism. While baptism is a requirement laid down in the Great Commission, it is "surrounded," as it were, by the disciple-making and teaching process. Finally, the content of the teaching is stated: "Obey everything I have commanded you" (verse 20). The Great Commission is therefore central to world mission, and the teaching of all the commands of Jesus is likewise central.[6]

Worldwide mission a sign of the Advent

The Great Commission ends with a promise: "I am with you always, to the very end of the age" (verse 20). According to Jesus, the age of the gospel to the world will come to an end, with the end of the world as it now is. Jesus also declared, "This gospel of the kingdom will be preached in the whole world as a testimony to all nations, and then the end will come" (Matthew 24:14). The main event marking the end is the visible return of Christ to this world in power and glory (verse 30). This event takes center place in the teaching of Jesus and the New Testament apostles about the future.

Conclusion

God's mission to save this world has stages, and the central stage involved the Incarnation—God entering this world in human form in the person of Jesus Christ. The Old Testament "come!" stage of mission in which people came to Jerusalem to learn of God came to a close during, and as a result of, the ministry of Jesus. He then launched the "go!" stage, in which His disciples would go out, first to fellow Jews, and then to Gentiles. In His commissioning of the disciples for world mission, Jesus left instructions about the importance of teaching and its content. Finally, He promised His continual presence with His disciples in mission, until they have succeeded in taking the gospel to the world. Then He will return in power and glory to introduce fully the promised rule of God.

---

1. Hebrew for "anointed one"—Israelite kings and high priests were among the "anointed ones" of that society.

2. Hebrew for "God with us."

3. The Hebrew word 'ōth translated "sign" has as one of its meanings, "omen foretelling the future." It also has this meaning in 2 Kings 20:8–10, where it refers to the shadow going backward ten steps, a sign involving the light of another heavenly body, the sun.

4. This daily statement of belief included Deuteronomy 6:4–9; 11:13–21; and Numbers 15:37–41. While only adult men were required to repeat it, women and children would certainly be familiar with it, because it directed fathers to "impress them [the commandments of God] on your children." "Talking about them when you sit at home" (Deuteronomy 6:7; 11:19).

5. The origins of this Jewish statement of fundamental beliefs, known as "The Eighteen," is not known. Daniel prayed an early form of it at his open window three times each day (Daniel 6:11).

6. For further insights on the Great Commission, see J. Herbert Kane, *Christian Missions in Biblical Perspective* (Grand Rapids, MI: Baker, 1976), 45–49.

CHAPTER

Jesus Reaches Out to the Gentiles

In popular speech, many people divide the human family into two groups: those "like us" and those "not like us." The ancient Greeks did this. They used the word *barbarian* for all non-Greeks. Likewise, Jews referred to non-Jews using the Hebrew word *goy.* Adventists sometimes do the same with the term *non-Adventist.* The English Bible uses Gentile, from the Latin *gentīlis,* to express the Jewish way of referring to non-Jewish persons. Lesson 8 sketches some ways Jesus refocused His mission and prepared His followers for the spread of the gospel to the Gentile world of "every nation, tribe, language, and people." He did this in response to the opposition of Jewish leaders, who made clear that they would not accept a role for the nation as a whole in God's mission to the world.

Many of Jesus' parables spoke to every nationality. This was especially true while He preached in Galilee, which even in Old Testament times was known as "Galilee of the nations" (Isaiah 9:1) because of its multicultural mix. Whether Jew or Gentile, Galilean farmers would get the point of His planting and harvesting parables. Those images drawn from everyday life in house and marketplace spoke equally clearly to all nationalities.

Other parables, however, hinted that Jewish leaders would reject their nation's role in the second stage of God's mission, forcing God to bypass them and appeal directly to the Gentiles. The parable of the king's wedding banquet, one of the most detailed and lengthy in the Gospels, focuses on this point with intense bluntness (Matthew 22:1–14; Luke 14:16–24). Jesus wove the same warning message into His parables of the workers in the vineyard (Matthew 20:1–16) and of the lost sheep (Matthew 18:12–14).

Jesus sometimes stated directly the message of these "refusal" parables: "Many will come from the east and the west, and will take their places at the feast with Abraham, Isaac and Jacob in the kingdom of heaven. But the subjects of the kingdom will be thrown outside, into the darkness, where there will be weeping and gnashing of teeth" (Matthew 8:11, 12).

Jews and Samaritans

No study of the mission outreach of Jesus is complete unless it deals with the Samaritans. This week's lesson for Sunday focuses on the Samaritan woman, and Wednesday's lesson on the Samaritan leper. Samaritans and Jews shared much history and heritage. They probably shared genes as well. Samaritans believed themselves to be descendants of the tribes of Ephraim and Manasseh. This was reflected in the words of the Samaritan woman to Jesus, when she referred to *our* father Jacob" (John 4:12, emphasis added). Jews had a different explanation for the origin of Samaritans: they believed them to be descendants of Gentiles brought into Israelite territory by the conquering Assyrians before 700 B.C. Some of these soldiers stayed and later intermarried with the Israelites.[1]

Samaritans worshiped one God, referred to regularly as Yahweh. Their Bible consisted of the five books of Moses and survives to this day in a version nearly identical to the Hebrew version of the same books. In the same way they were to Jews, Abraham, Jacob, and Moses were important ancestors to Samaritans. Samaritans claimed the support of the Persian king Darius for their temple, which they built on Mount Gerizim, about forty-three miles (seventy kilometers) north of Jerusalem. It was destroyed in 128 B.C. by a Jewish high priest and king at the head of a Jewish army. As payback, Samaritans sometimes attacked groups of Jewish pilgrims on their way to Jerusalem. One time, before the birth of Jesus, Samaritans sneaked into the Jerusalem temple and scattered bones, making it unclean for worship.

Samaritans and Jews were rivals, not because they were so different, but because they had much in common. They were related genetically, geographically, culturally, and spiritually. But they were divided by centuries of competition, hatred, and periods of warfare—all the ingredients needed to make Samaria a tough mission field for the Jewish Jesus and His disciples. The Gospels record two stages of Jesus' Samaritan mission—the woman at the well and the Samaritan leper.

The Samaritan woman

The cultural tension of the story of Jesus and the Samaritan woman is expressed by the words of John 4:9: "For Jews do not associate with Samaritans." The footnote to this verse in the New International Version suggests a different translation: "[Jews] do not use dishes Samaritans have used." Another recent translation's footnote reads, "[Jews] won't use the same cups" (CEV).

Like the Jews, Samaritans expected the Messiah. One of the main biblical signs to help them identify the true Messiah was stated in Deuteronomy 18:18: "He [the Messiah] will *tell them everything*" (emphasis added). The Samaritan woman knew this verse. It was clear from her statement in her conversation with Jesus: "When he [Messiah] comes, he will *explain everything*" (John 4:25; emphasis added). When she rushed back to the village after talking with Jesus, she called out, Come, see a man who "*told me everything*" (verse 39; emphasis added). By uttering these words she was transformed from "the Samaritan woman" into "pioneer Samaritan evangelist" for Jesus, announcing that the one who would *tell them everything* had arrived!

The Roman army officer

During the early part of His ministry, Jesus carried out a passive mission to the Gentiles but stopped short of an active mission. When Gentiles came asking for healing, Jesus did not refuse. He honored their requests according to their faith. It must have taken great faith for a Gentile to approach Jesus. When a Roman army captain in Capernaum appealed to Jesus to heal his servant, Jesus praised the captain's faith even before He did the requested healing (Matthew 8:5–13; Luke 7:1–10). He did not visit the centurion's house, because for Him to enter a Gentile home at that point in His ministry could have created a barrier between Him and some fellow Jews.

This healing story has two high points. The first is the healing of the servant. But the second is what Jesus revealed about the centurion's faith—"such great faith" He had not found in Israel. The centurion's faith was visible, practical, and lasting. This is clear from what the Jewish community leaders reported to Jesus about him: "He loves our nation and has built our synagogue" (Luke 7:5). The centurion probably did not attend synagogue every Sabbath because of his army officer status and its work demands. He probably did not convert to Judaism—army regulations probably did not allow it. But his heart was opened to the God of Israel, and his generous deeds made him, in their opinion, a "righteous Gentile." This man was not far from the kingdom.

Demon-afflicted man and woman outside Jewish territory

With the healing of the demon-possessed men (or man, according to Mark and Luke) of Gadara, a pattern emerges in the mission strategy of Jesus. When traveling outside Jewish territory, Jesus engaged with local persons who then, by first-hand personal testimony about His healing actions, spread the gospel among their own people more effectively than He or His Jewish disciples could.

First, we have the demon-afflicted man of Gadara. The first three Gospels devote a total of fifty-one verses to this mission trip on the eastern side of the Sea of Galilee. It was clearly important for Jesus' mission to Gentiles. One striking feature of this story is the large herd of pigs and their herders. Like dogs, pigs are scavengers, well suited to cleaning up just about anything organic that they find as they browse. But they cannot survive on a diet of grass alone. Herds of wild pigs were, and still are, a problem in little-inhabited areas of the Middle

East and in other countries. Non-Jewish people, especially those on low incomes, raised pigs as food. Pigs were also used for sacrifices in many religions in the ancient world. The fact that Jews did not eat pigs or sacrifice them made them stand out as different from most of their neighbors. This particular herd of two thousand pigs was not wild but farmed, as we can tell when the Gospels refer to the action of their herders when the pigs rushed into the water.

By His healing action, and His negotiating with demons to enter the pigs, Jesus confronted the local people with a chance to free themselves from pagan beliefs and from their unclean animals, and remove the presence among them of powerful demons. They looked at their demon-possessed neighbor in his restored state—healed, clothed, and in his right mind. They also noted the sudden loss of their pigs.

They had to make a choice, and they did, asking Jesus to leave. Because the loss of two thousand pigs dominated their thoughts, the people could not see the blessing of healing of one of their own. Meanwhile, the healed man wanted to join Jesus, but he was told, according to Mark's and Luke's accounts, to stay with his own people and simply tell what the Lord had done for him (Mark 5:19, 20; Luke 8:39).

Jesus' mission strategy was at work here. He "planted" a witness to the power of the gospel who spoke the language and knew the culture. According to Mark, the healed man visited at least ten towns (which is the meaning of the Greek word *Decapolis* in Mark 5:20) with his personal testimony about the before-and-after change to his life performed by God through Jesus.

The other story is the demon-afflicted girl of Sidon. How would Jesus treat a truly Gentile woman who was not even Samaritan? The Gospels answer this question by the story of a Canaanite woman in the region of Tyre and Sidon who came to Jesus, pleading for Him to heal her daughter (Matthew 15:21–28). It would be hard to find a person with lower status. She was a female Canaanite requesting healing for a female child. Each of these labels contributes to communicating the low status of the persons involved.

The mother repeated her request over and over, and prostrated herself at Jesus' feet. After ignoring her, He finally answered, telling her that He had been sent to the lost sheep of the house of Israel only. He then chose a negative ethnic label, which he applied to her and her people, comparing them to dogs on the floor, while referring to His own people as children eating at the table.

She did not allow herself to be insulted by this ethnic label. She accepted it for the moment and turned it into a further plea by pointing out that in grand houses where people eat meals at tables, it was the custom to bring in dogs to clean up any food dropped onto the floor. Did she somehow understand that Jesus' healing mission to the Jews would soon begin to spread to Gentiles? Or was she simply a deeply devoted mother willing to try anything for her little girl?

Jesus was impressed by her determination and her faith. "Woman, you have great faith!" (verse 28). He then healed her daughter. She got home to find her daughter freed from the demon, a reward for her faith. What she did not understand was that this signaled that Jesus' mission would include Gentiles as well as Jews and Samaritans, women as well as men, and children as well as adults.

Jesus' ministry to the Gentiles was motivated by Old Testament prophecies, which made clear that, through the Messiah, God would reach out to Gentiles. The first of the prophet Isaiah's "Servant of the Lord" prophecies stated God's plan for the Gentiles, through the ministry of His Servant: "Here is my servant, whom I uphold, my chosen one in whom I delight; I will put my Spirit on him, and he will bring justice to the nations" (Isaiah 42:1). "He will not falter or be discouraged till he establishes justice on earth. In his law the islands will put their trust" (verse 4); "I will keep you [my Servant] and will make you to be a covenant for the people and a light for the Gentiles" (verse 6); "I will also make you a light to the Gentiles, that my salvation may reach to the ends of the earth" (Isaiah 49:6).

Jesus' fellow Jews, who knew these "Servant" prophecies, could not doubt that the salvation prophesied there would go to the Gentiles. It was only a matter of time.

A Samaritan with leprosy

One of ten lepers who called out to Jesus as He walked on the border between Samaria and Galilee was Samaritan (Luke 17:11–19). The other nine were Jews. The border between Samaria and Galilee was not clearly marked, except on the main roads, where customs would have been collected. In what could have been a sort of no-man's-land between the regions was a village, part of which had been set aside as a leper colony. As Jesus passed, some of the lepers in that sad place recognized Him and started calling for His attention and mercy. He sent them to see the priests, who had responsibility for declaring lepers cleansed (see Leviticus 14). Did the Samaritan leper present himself to the Jewish priest? Or to a Samaritan priest? Would a Jewish priest deal with a Samaritan? Would the priest even know whether the leper standing before him was Samaritan? These questions are not answered.

A major purpose for this story is to declare that the mission of Jesus was about to take its first step beyond the Jewish people. It is one of a collection of Gospel accounts naming Samaritans. They help us to track the ethnic expansion of Jesus' mission. Was this Samaritan leper being prepared as another missionary to his own people, following the pattern of the woman at the well? It would soon become clear, when the apostle Philip began his mission to Samaria, that the Samaritans had been prepared in advance for the good news about Jesus as the Messiah (Acts 8:4–8).

Greeks request to see Jesus

Major milestones mark the earthly ministry of Jesus. The Gospel of John draws attention to them by use of Jesus' expression, "my hour." At the wedding in Cana (John 2:4, ESV), He declared, "My hour has not yet come." Later, when He taught in the temple court, two attempts were made to arrest Him (John 7:30; 8:20). Both failed because "his hour had not yet come."

But His hour arrived near the end of His ministry. Jesus declared it when a group of Greek pilgrims in Jerusalem for Passover approached the disciple Philip with a request: "We would like to see Jesus" (John 12:21). When Jesus learned of their request, He declared: "The hour has come for the Son of Man to be glorified" (verse 23). What caused this change? How did the request from a band of Greek-speaking pilgrims to Jerusalem reveal to Jesus that a crucial hour, a turning point in His mission, had come?

Isaiah 66 contains a prophecy that revealed that an important step in His mission, His hour, had come. Here are the key words: "I will set a sign among them, and I will send some of those who survived to the nations—to Tarshish, to the Libyans and Lydians . . . , to Tubal and Greece, and to the distant islands that have not heard of my fame or seen my glory" (Isaiah 66:19). These Greeks, waiting to see Jesus, were a fulfillment of the sign that the Lord promised through Isaiah.

These Greeks, like thousands of others in Jerusalem for Passover, would soon "see the Lord's glory" in the arrest, crucifixion, and especially the resurrection of Jesus. They had been guided to Jerusalem at the right time. When Jesus learned of their arrival, He understood that His hour had come and that He would soon become the ultimate Passover Lamb. These Greek pilgrims would be among those witnesses from many nations who would be sent back home to "proclaim" the Lord's glory among the nations, just as Isaiah prophesied.

Conclusion

Jesus lived, at one level, within the strict ethnic beliefs and customs of His fellow Jews. But at another level, He showed awareness that the gospel to the Gentiles was the all-important next stage of God's mission. He tried to prepare His people, and especially their leaders, to follow God's lead and assist in taking the gospel to the Gentiles. But they refused. Jesus continued to work, meeting the requests of selected Gentiles who approached Him. Eventually, in parables and teachings, Jesus began to point out the place Gentiles would have in God's salvation. He followed this with engagement of the Gentiles, healing them and leaving them in their communities as eyewitnesses to His power as they worked for this new stage of world mission.

---

1. This section draws on Robert T. Anderson, "Samaritans," in *Anchor Bible Dictionary,* ed. David Noel Freedman (New York: Doubleday, 1992), 5:941–947.

CHAPTER

Peter: Conservative Missionary Leader

Simon, son of John, fisherman from Bethsaida in Galilee, became the disciple Peter. His name appears more than 150 times in the New Testament and is on nearly every page of the Gospels, all of which signals his role as lead disciple and apostle. Peter was spokesperson, leader among the disciples, and chief eyewitness to Jesus' resurrection.

He was first among the disciples in many ways: first called by Jesus (Matthew 4:18; John 1:42); first to confess Jesus to be the Messiah (Matthew 16:16); first to rebuke Jesus for speaking of His coming death (verse 22); first to speak up during Jesus' transfiguration (Matthew 17:4); first to deny Jesus (Matthew 26:69–75); first to enter the empty tomb (Luke 24:12); first to heal in the name of Jesus after the Day of Pentecost (Acts 3:6); first to preach to temple worshipers (Acts 3:12); first to be arrested for his testimony (Acts 4:3); first to stand before the Jewish ruling council (verse 7); first to witness to a Gentile, Cornelius (Acts 10:1, 24–28).

Peter's closeness to Jesus and his willingness to get involved made him eyewitness to all the important events in the ministry of Jesus. As eyewitness to so much of what Jesus did, Peter was in the strongest position of any of the disciples to testify to the truth about Jesus.

Building bridges: Starting from Jerusalem

The gift of sharing the gospel in various languages on the Day of Pentecost liberated Christianity from the need to privilege one language, which alone would be expected to contain and express its message. On that day the Holy Spirit made clear that the Christian message could be expressed in any human language. The gift of hearing on the Day of Pentecost, in the listener's own language, "the mighty works of God" (Acts 2:11, ESV) marked another stage in God's mission plan.

A person's native language is a powerful medium for stirring the emotions and triggering the will to take action. For this reason, people need to hear the gospel in their own language. Christian mission today needs to resist privileging one language above others in efforts to spread the gospel. While Seventh-day Adventists are multilingual, proclaiming the gospel in 892 languages, the known languages in today's world are nearly 6,900 in number. For us, English remains our "official" language. Church leaders not fluent in English lose chances to influence other leaders, even when their ideas may be valuable. Especially in mission, we must always be diligent to make the gospel available in the languages of the people.

Peter's Pentecost sermon became a pattern that the apostles and their helpers followed wherever they traveled to proclaim Jesus. Peter opened by proclaiming Bible prophecy was being fulfilled that very morning as the Spirit of God was poured out on Jesus' followers. He then used the Psalms and personal testimony to reveal the true identity of Jesus, the purpose of His ministry and crucifixion, and His new status as Lord and Christ at God's right hand. While there is no direct mention of Christ's return in Peter's Pentecost sermon, it was an important part of his later sermons, as is clear in Acts 3:20, 21. Peter's sermon ended with an appeal to listeners to repent and receive forgiveness.

The Day of Pentecost also saw fulfillment of the prophecy of Daniel 7:14: "He [the Son of man] was given authority, glory and sovereign power; all nations and peoples of every language worshiped him." By sunset on the Day of Pentecost, three thousand Jewish pilgrims from as many as fifteen nations (according to Acts 2:9–11) entered, through repentance and baptism, the kingdom of the Son of man—a very good result for the first Christian mission effort, and convincing fulfillment of Old Testament prophecies that Jews dispersed across the world would be blessed and enlightened on their return to Jerusalem.

Peter as missionary inspector in Samaria

Jesus gave authority to the disciples as a group before sending them on their first mission trip (Matthew 10:1–4). So while Jesus foretold a special place for Peter when He told him, "You are Peter, and on this rock I will build my church" (Matthew 16:18), the New Testament does not present Peter as head of the church. Peter took the initiative many times. He was often first to speak at major episodes in Jesus' ministry. His regrettable denials at Jesus' trial marked a serious failure (Matthew 26:69–75). He needed to be recommissioned after that failure. It happened when the risen Christ, after confirming Peter's love for Him, commissioned him to "take care of my sheep" (John 21:16) and "follow me" (verse 19).

After Jesus' ascension, Peter continued to be first to speak. He did so when the disciples chose a replacement for Judas (Acts 1:15–26), and he delivered the sermon on the Day of Pentecost, although he was backed by the eleven (Acts 2:14–40). Peter spoke in support of baptizing Gentiles without first requiring them to become Jews. He delivered the deciding speech at the Jerusalem Council (Acts 15:7–11).

But Peter was clearly not in charge back at Jerusalem headquarters. He and the other disciples, now known as apostles, worked as a group, setting a pattern for making group leadership decisions about church matters. When increasing numbers of believers in Jerusalem brought complaints about fair food distribution between the Hebrew-speaking and Greek-speaking believers, the twelve apostles solved the problem as a group (Acts 6:1–6). When the first council was held in Jerusalem, James the brother of Jesus, not Peter, was in charge (Acts 15:13–21).

When reports of a rapid increase of believers in Samaria reached Jerusalem headquarters, the apostles collectively decided to send Peter and John. The reason for their visit was to recognize and affirm Philip's evangelistic work and pray the Holy Spirit onto the new believers. Peter and John had been with Jesus during His pioneering mission to Samaria (John 4:1–42). Their experience as eyewitnesses to Jesus' mission during their two days in a Samaritan village would aid them in guiding and settling the new Samaritan believers. And they could fill in any gaps in Philip's theology and teaching of the Christian message.

Cornelius, Roman army officer

The Roman army was present and visible nearly everywhere in the world of the New Testament, including Judea. Because of repeated objections by the Jews in Jerusalem to the Roman army being headquartered in that city, it was located instead in Caesarea, about seventy miles (110 kilometers) northwest of Jerusalem, on the coast. Roman soldiers in territory with a Jewish population tended to support the enemies of the Jews during any uprising. It was therefore unusual for a soldier to be friendly to Jews and follow their religion. Like nearly all centurions (the word means "commander of one hundred soldiers"), Cornelius would have been a Roman citizen and a Gentile. Though stationed in Judea, he was possibly retired by the time of Peter's visit. His devotion to God, generosity to the synagogue, and prayer help readers understand that he was searching for God through the Jewish faith.

The early followers of Jesus would have been especially uneasy in the presence of soldiers of the Judean cohort, who were the ones who carried out the crucifixion of Jesus barely ten years earlier. Was it possible—no one really knows—that Cornelius had been on duty in Jerusalem that day? God had worked for years preparing Cornelius for his role in the mission to Gentiles, and it was now time for the next step. Through an angel God directed Cornelius to send messengers to Joppa to invite Peter. The unfolding of this amazing story, the longest in the book of Acts, must have astonished both Peter and Cornelius and those with them.

Peter and the unclean animals

Peter's side of this story opens in the city of Joppa, the port where the prophet Jonah boarded a ship to flee from his mission assignment hundreds of years earlier (Jonah 1:3). Joppa was the port city for goods and travelers going to and from Jerusalem and Judea, so it had a mainly Jewish population. This must have seemed to Peter a good place for contacting fellow Jews as they traveled to and from points farther west, south, and north. He stayed for some time on the edge of the city with a Jew named Simon, a tanner.

Tanning animal skins to make leather was an important industry, but it was antisocial. In the tanning process, the animal hides were treated with animal and human waste. Tanners were for that reason also collectors of such waste and provided a door-to-door service for people living nearby. While someone had to do it, tanners had low social status as a result of this part of their work. Tanneries were not allowed within the cities. This is why the instructions to the Roman centurion Cornelius for finding Peter included the information, "He is staying with Simon the tanner, whose house is by the sea" (Acts 10:6).

At this stage of mission the question "Can a Gentile become a Christian without first becoming a Jew?" had not been answered. God's strategy behind this step was carefully worked out. Peter's preparation included the successful mission to Samaria, which built on Jesus' own pioneering Samaritan mission. But Samaritans were not full Gentiles. What happened as Peter waited on the roof for something to eat was so important for Christian mission that it is reported twice, in almost identical words, in Acts 10:9–16 and 11:5–10.

Peter received a vision "in a trance" of a sheet lowered to earth, filled with the full range of animals that God created to populate water, air, and land during days five and six of Creation week (Genesis 1:20–25). He said, "I now realize how true it is that God does not show favoritism but accepts from every nation the one who fears him and does what is right" (Acts 10:34, 35). The labels "clean" and "unclean" were applied to animals by God at the time of the Flood (Genesis 7:2). This difference between clean and unclean animals had become a very important part of Hebrew faith and Hebrew diet (Leviticus 11). It also influenced services at the temple in Jerusalem, because only clean animals were accepted by God as sacrificial offerings (started already by Noah; Genesis 8:20), and only clean animals could be used as food.

Peter was shocked by the command in his vision to "get up, . . . kill and eat" (Acts 10:13; 11:7). He protested, declaring his faithful obedience to God's instruction to avoid unclean animals. The command was repeated three times. The message was clear: God had declared "clean" what Jews for many generations understood to be unclean. As Peter reflected on this vision, visitors arrived, asking for him. Another voice, this time the Holy Spirit's, commanded him: "Get up!" But it was not to kill and eat but rather to go with those visitors.

Peter came to understand that his vision was not about animals and food but about people. His first words to Cornelius and his household show the enormous cultural and spiritual deepening of Peter's thinking between the tanner's rooftop and the centurion's doorstep, where he declared: "You are well aware that it is against our law for a Jew to associate with or visit a Gentile" (Acts 10:28). God poured out the Holy Spirit on Cornelius and his family, confirming the correctness of Peter's realization that, for followers of Jesus, all people are "clean" and can be approached with the gospel. "I now realize how true it is that God does not show favoritism but accepts from every nation the one who fears him and does what is right" (verses 34, 35).

Two main lessons about Christian mission were woven into this episode. The lesson for Peter and believers was that the gospel is for all classes and ethnic groups. The lesson for Cornelius and his family was that family name, position, even godliness in the eyes of the synagogue, were not enough. For salvation, they needed to learn of Jesus as sacrifice for sins, judge, source of forgiveness and eternal life. And they needed baptism by the Holy Spirit and by water. Finally, they needed several days of instruction from Peter and fellow believers.

The Jerusalem decree

Meanwhile, back at headquarters, the apostles and other believers awaited a report of Peter's latest mission. Imagine their astonishment at reports that "the Gentiles also had received the word of God" (Acts 11:1). It was now the turn of leaders at mission headquarters to understand this new stage of mission, already experienced by Peter and his companions in Caesarea. The leaders had not been there to witness for themselves the outpouring of the Spirit directly onto Gentiles. They had to believe or disbelieve the testimony of Peter, backed up by the "believers from Joppa," who were there (Acts 10:23, 45).

Organizations and movements are healthier when time and place are provided for discussion and debate about important issues. Church leaders at mission headquarters in Jerusalem realized the need for discussion and debate about the entry of Gentiles; thus, they arranged to examine the issue. The meeting reported in Acts 15 was the church's first "General Conference session." It had a single agenda item: *Do Gentile converts have to become Jews in order to become Christians?*

Speakers for both sides of the issue met and debated. Both sides were given a hearing. Paul, Barnabas, and believers from the church in Antioch spoke against the requirement of circumcision for Gentile converts, while some believers, with a Pharisee background, spoke for it. The apostles and leading elders listened and conducted their own vigorous discussion. Then they listened to Peter's story of the outpouring of the Spirit on the uncircumcised Gentile family of Cornelius in Caesarea. This was followed by testimony from Paul and Barnabas about signs and wonders done among their uncircumcised converts.

The leaders then declared their decision, and they did it through their spokesperson, the apostle James, brother of Jesus (Galatians 1:19) and "pillar" of the Jerusalem church (Galatians 2:9). He quoted the prophecy of Amos 9, which declared there would be a place in a restored Israel for Gentiles (Acts 15:13–17). Then he stated his "judgment" that circumcision not be required of Gentile converts, but that they should observe some important lifestyle practices that would make it easier for Jewish believers to mix with them.

By following this procedure, the early church set an example of allowing open discussion, even vigorous argument (Acts 15:2, 7); of following a representative form of church leadership; and of basing decisions on careful study of Scripture (only the Old Testament at that time) along with the example and teaching of Jesus. The Holy Spirit thus led the church into the new stage of mission and to tolerance on matters not essential for believing Gentiles.

Conclusion: Peter's letters to diaspora Jews and pagan converts

For Peter, the most up-to-date and effective means of mass communication over time and distance was by letter. Like other New Testament authors, Peter wrote letters to exercise pastoral care, encourage mission work, and administer churches in the growing mission fields. The two letters in his name were carried across the scattered territories of the Roman world by personal friends and were read aloud in many gatherings of Christians.

In his letters, Peter encouraged Gentile believers to enjoy their new-found status and relation to God, which in former times was available only to Israelites: "You are a chosen people [echoing Deuteronomy 7:6], a royal priesthood [echoing Exodus 19:6], a holy nation [echoing Exodus 19:6], a people belonging to God [echoing Exodus 19:5]" (1 Peter 2:9). The socially conservative Peter then urged readers to live in such a way that unbelievers would be won to Christ: "Live such good lives among the pagans that, though they accuse you of doing wrong, they may see your good deeds and glorify God on the day he visits us" (verse 12).

Peter next suggested that Christians live, so far as possible, in harmony with governments and rulers (verses 13–17), and that they relate to one another, as far as possible, within their community's social customs, including even slavery and the limited place assigned to married women (verses 18–3:6). The goal of Christian slaves and wives should be to win others by their Christlike demeanor.

Peter's administrative role is seen in the advice he gave to local pastors. He reminded them that his leadership was a result of his role as eyewitness of Christ's suffering and resurrection (1 Peter 5:1). They were to pastor because they chose to and because they were eager to serve. They should not profit dishonestly from their position (verse 2), and they should lead their church by good example, "not lording it over those entrusted" to them (verse 3).

Finally, Peter cautioned all believers that the devil could and should be resisted, even though he was like a roaring lion. Present temptation and suffering would not last long. God would soon make them "strong, firm and steadfast" (verse 10).

The closing instruction in Peter's second letter reflected his own deepening understanding of the grace of God, which he gained through years as disciple, apostle, missionary, and church leader: "Grow in the grace and knowledge of our Lord and Savior Jesus Christ. To him be glory both now and forever! Amen" (2 Peter 3:18).

Philip: Table Waiter Turned Missionary

This week's lesson covers the mission career of Philip, one of the seven original deacons serving the Jerusalem believers. This was not the disciple Philip, who was also an active missionary. This Philip, known as Philip the evangelist, first appears at a time of rapid growth and tension between believers who spoke Hebrew and Aramaic and those who spoke Greek (Acts 6:1). Increased numbers of believers as a result of the outpouring of the Holy Spirit on the Day of Pentecost strained the practical housekeeping arrangements the apostles had put in place for the believers in Jerusalem (Acts 2:46; 4:32–35). Complaints arose that Greek-speaking widows were being overlooked when food was distributed (Acts 6:1).[1]

From their earliest days, Christians have been concerned not just with people's spiritual needs, but with their material and social needs as well, a concern inherited from Jesus. The Twelve Apostles solved the tension by appointing seven men to meet physical and social needs. This freed the Twelve to continue their focus on the core spiritual matters of the Christian faith—prayer and God's Word (verse 4).

As one of the seven deacons appointed to solve this problem, Philip is presented as a flexible person who loved to share Christ and who also adapted to change. His recorded mission work covered about twenty-five years and took him from Jerusalem to Samaria, Gaza, and finally Caesarea—a distance of about 170 miles (274 kilometers). His name means "loves horses," but he probably walked most of that distance, except for one time when the Spirit "suddenly took Philip away" (Acts 8:39).

This week's lesson includes a rare glimpse into Philip's home, his four prophesying daughters, and his hospitality, especially to a former enemy of Christ.

Philip: Willing and adaptable missionary

Following directions of the apostles, the believers chose seven men with the right qualifications. Luke named these qualifications: (1) honest; (2) full of the Spirit; and (3) wise. They had to speak Greek and understand the culture and customs of the Greek-speaking Jews and converts to the Jewish faith. The apostles then commissioned them, including Philip, by prayer and laying-on of hands (Acts 6:6).

It is important to note that while the seven were chosen to administer the fair distribution of food, their service soon grew beyond "waiting on tables" (verse 1) into the heart of all Christian mission work: proclaiming the gospel. This should alert Christians to the need for balance in mission. Though it is easier to hear the gospel on a full stomach, meeting the physical needs of people must not be allowed to silence the proclamation, to become in itself the church's mission. Even those whose main task is "waiting on tables" can and must proclaim the gospel in word as well as deed.

Receiving and believing eyewitness testimony

Philip was apparently not an eyewitness of the main events in the life and ministry of Jesus. Like all other Christian believers not present at the main events in the life of Jesus, he depended on eyewitness testimony. New Testament authors reminded their readers that they depended on testimony "handed down to us by those who from the first were eyewitnesses" (Luke 1:2). This eyewitness testimony was of central importance: "We must pay the most careful attention, therefore, to what we have heard [from eyewitnesses]" (Hebrews 2:1).

But the fact that Philip and most other early believers were not eyewitnesses did not compromise their faith or make them second-class believers. On the contrary, Jesus had pronounced a blessing on all those who believed without themselves being eyewitnesses: "Blessed are those who have not seen and yet have believed" (John 20:29; see also 17:20). Nor did it make them second-class missionaries.

Philip's missionary qualifications and credentials did not come about by accident. He, like others, was chosen by God, who directed his life events so he was in the right places at the right times to gain the qualifications and experience needed for pioneering Christian mission. Under God's guidance, Philip was part of a Greek-speaking community. He was brought to Jerusalem at the right time to learn of Jesus and to become a believer. God further qualified him by filling him with the Holy Spirit and with wisdom. Finally, God completed his qualifications for mission by prompting his fellow believers to select him as one of the seven, and by directing the apostles to commission him for service—a bigger service than any of them foresaw at the time.

Religious borders are crossed: Philip in Samaria

Philip did not stay long in Jerusalem. He and the other Jerusalem believers, apart from the apostles, were "scattered" in the persecution that broke out the day his fellow deacon Stephen was stoned. "They were all scattered" (Acts 8:1, author's translation) implies that someone did the scattering. The Greek word here translated "scattered" is related to the verb "to sow seed." In other words, a careful reading of the passage shows Luke intended readers to understand that God did the scattering. These believers became the "scattered seed" of the gospel. To them at the time, their flight from Jerusalem must have seemed a personal trial and a setback for the gospel. But their scattering spread their testimony and led to the further increase of believers. It was a small but important step in the spread of the gospel to the very ends of the earth.

The refugee Philip went quickly to work evangelizing the Samaritan city where he settled. It was probably Sebaste, the chief city of Samaria, site of the capital city and royal residence of the northern kingdom of

Old Testament Israel. In Philip's day, Sebaste's city wall was two and a half miles (four kilometers) in length. According to tradition, Sebaste was the burial place of John the Baptist.

In a rapid series of action words, Luke described how the gospel message made the journey from Philip's lips to Samaritan hearts (verses 5, 6). He "proclaimed" publicly (Greek *kērussō*) the Christ—the recently crucified Jesus of Nazareth, God's promised and prophesied Messiah. "Crowds" of the city's inhabitants "paid close attention" to what he proclaimed. Then "with a united mind,"[2] they "listened."

Another feature of Philip's mission work was the powerful signs he did as the people watched (verses 6, 7). This was also a feature that accompanied Peter's preaching of the gospel, and it would later also become a part of Paul's mission.[3] The signs in Philip's ministry to that Samaritan city included freeing people from demon possession and healing the paralyzed and lame—the same signs reported earlier in the ministry of Peter (Acts 4:30). For a city troubled by powerful demons, the gospel truth that demons were subject to Jesus brought escape and freedom to many Samaritans.

In Luke's reports of conversions, three fundamental steps are included: repentance, baptism, and receiving the Holy Spirit. Peter named them in his Pentecost sermon: "Repent and be baptized, every one of you . . . and you will receive the gift of the Holy Spirit" (Acts 2:38; 3:19).

Repentance was always the first required step (Acts 2:38; 3:19; 8:22; 17:30; 26:20). Sometimes the Holy Spirit was named in second place, and baptism third, as in the household of Cornelius (Acts 10:47). At other times baptism was named in second place, and the Holy Spirit third (Acts 1:5; 19:1–6).

The exact nature of one of these three steps, the outpouring of the Holy Spirit, continues to be debated. It is important to note, however, the wording Luke used to state all three steps. "Repent!" is a command directed to a person under conviction of the Spirit, in response to apostolic preaching of the gospel. "Be baptized!" is also a specific command. The first command calls for a decision, an act of the will; that is, a change of attitude and belief about oneself and one's relationship to

God. If this first command is obeyed, the second one, "Be baptized!" then needs to obeyed as well.

It is important to understand that while these first and second steps are stated in the form of commands, there is no command to receive the gift of the Holy Spirit. Nowhere in Acts were believers *commanded* to receive the Spirit. Rather, the gift was a promise God made. No act of the human will could bring the Holy Spirit. So, in Acts, coming to belief in Jesus required two steps: "Repent!" and "Be baptized!" The public displays of the Spirit's power in Acts were part of the fulfillment of Jesus' promise to the disciples rather than a feature of the conversion of each individual. He told His disciples, "I am going to send you what my Father has promised; but stay in the city until you have been clothed with power from on high" (Luke 24:49).

Luke referred to Jesus' promise of "power from on high" in slightly different words in Acts 1:4, 5: "While he was eating with them, he gave them this command: 'Do not leave Jerusalem, but wait for the gift my Father promised. . . . In a few days you will be baptized with the Holy Spirit.' " The Father's promise began to be fulfilled on the Day of Pentecost.

Philip and the African: Toward the ends of the earth

"Get up and travel!" (Acts 8:26, author's translation). With these words, echoing the command to Abram long before, Philip's mission field suddenly changes from Samaria in the north to the busy road from Jerusalem to Gaza. Like Abram, Philip got up and went (verse 27), not quite sure where or why. He had no idea, as he stood on the side of that main road between two continents, that soon he would help spread the gospel to Africa.

Ethiopia—Cush in the Old Testament—fascinated ancient Europeans and western Asians. To Greeks, the name meant "land of the burnt-face people." According to one Greek author, Ethiopians were known to be long-lived, the tallest, and most handsome of peoples.[4] There was regular travel and trade between Ethiopia and the Roman world in the first century A.D., so an Ethiopian dignitary visiting Jerusalem was not surprising, even though the distance was as much as twelve hundred miles (two thousand kilometers)! Cush was named in Psalm 68 as one of the nations that would come to know the true God:

> Summon your power, God;
>> show us your strength, our God, as you have done before.
> Because of your temple at Jerusalem
>> kings will bring you gifts. . . .
> Envoys will come from Egypt;
>> Cush will submit herself to God.
> Sing to God, you kingdoms of the earth,
>> sing praise to the Lord (Psalm 68:28, 29, 31, 32).

Surprisingly, Luke did not give us the Ethiopian's name, but only his nationality and position in his queen's government. He was well educated. As Philip ran alongside the chariot he heard him reading aloud from the scroll of Isaiah (many cultures even today read aloud). He most likely had learned Hebrew as part of becoming a convert to Judaism. That would help to explain his visit to Jerusalem. Many cultured pagans across the ancient world appreciated what the Jews had— high moral standards, dietary practices that aided health, freedom from idolatry. Some actually joined Judaism in order to fully benefit from these social and spiritual advantages. The Ethiopian was probably a convert.

When Philip heard him reading Isaiah's prophecy of the suffering Servant of the Lord, it gave the entry point he needed for the first Christian Bible study conducted in a moving chariot (Acts 8:31). The Holy Spirit must have been at work on the Ethiopian for some time, because after getting answers to his question and hearing Philip's Bible study, he requested baptism, right there on the spot. After his baptism, the Ethiopian "went on his way rejoicing" (verse 39) and Philip was "snatched away" by the Lord (see verse 40).

In Judea: Philip as evangelist, father, and host

When not "on the road" (see Acts 8:5, 26–30, 39, 40) in his mission work, Philip was at home in Caesarea (Acts 8:40; 21:8), where we meet him, twenty-five years after he was appointed deacon back in Jerusalem. Home life for the families of evangelists and missionaries is often challenging because of frequent and sometimes very long absences. Luke was aware of ancient Greek literature and drama, read and acted on the stages of cities across the empire, which focused on the struggles of wives and children back home while heads of household were away on extended journeys or army duty.

Even with an extended family to provide support, home life is stressed when the head of household is away. Another source of family suffering arises from spiritual attacks on Christian workers and their families. One way to hinder the spread of the gospel is to injure it by turning the hearts of the children of evangelists and missionaries against the faith. According to the Old Testament's closing prophecy, Malachi 4:5, 6, one task of the promised returning prophet Elijah would be to turn the hearts of fathers to their children and the hearts of children to their fathers.

Philip's family coped with his absences and survived any spiritual attacks on them. This is clear because at home with Philip were his four unmarried, prophesying daughters. Like their father, they engaged in Spirit-guided ministry. The apostle Paul would have experienced their ministry during his extended stay in their home (Acts 21:8–10). Paul had earlier written praising the gift of prophecy, stating it was more valuable than tongues for Christian believers because it built up believers and their congregations (1 Corinthians 14:1–5).

"Be reconciled!"

The power of the gospel to reconcile people is demonstrated by Paul's stay in Philip's home. Twenty-five years earlier, Paul, known then as Saul, eagerly supported fellow Jews as they stoned Stephen, Philip's fellow deacon in the Jerusalem church. Saul then took the lead in a wave of persecution that sent Philip and fellow believers fleeing for their lives from Jerusalem. Under the life-changing impact of his encounter with the living Jesus on the Damascus road, a hate-filled Saul was turned into a leading apostle of Jesus and chief missionary to the Gentiles.

Now, years later, Paul entered Philip's home as a guest, staying "a number of days" (Acts 21:10). Philip and Paul had become reconciled. Now united in service to Christ, these two former enemies shared table fellowship, something that would have been impossible before Saul's conversion. Reconciliation was one of the ministries God gave His people (2 Corinthians 5:18), and those days together in Caesarea helped believers see for themselves how Philip and Paul lived the reconciled life.

After this glimpse into his home in Caesarea, Philip disappears from the pages of the New Testament. He served God faithfully as deacon, missionary to Samaria and other non-Jewish territories, and evangelist. He was the first New Testament person to carry that title (Acts 21:8). As missionary he launched Christian mission to the continent of Africa through his brief encounter with the Ethiopian. In addition to these mission exploits he was blessed by a believing family and by a spirit of hospitality to fellow missionaries.

Conclusion

Philip served God's mission plan as table waiter, refugee, and traveling evangelist. He played an important part in the transition of mission method from "come" to "go," and he was very effective in cross-cultural communication. Through him the Holy Sprit worked powerfully to heal people and free them in the name of Jesus from demonic influence. He also did pioneering work when he proclaimed the gospel to an African. Finally, he maintained a home life that nurtured his family and that empowered his prophesying daughters to achieve their role, as promised by the prophet Joel: "Your sons and daughters will prophesy" (Acts 2:17).

---

1. This passage echoes the complaining and murmuring of the hungry Israelites in the wilderness, which led to the gift of manna in Exodus 16:1–7.

2. Luke uses the Greek word *homothumadon* here and several other places in Acts to express a special type of group unity that pulsed through gatherings of early believers, from the day of Jesus' ascension (Acts 1:15) and through the rest of Acts.

3. See Acts 2:22, 43; 4:16, 22, 30; 5:12; 6:8; 8:6, 13; 14:3; 15:12.

4. Herodotus, *The Histories,* bk. 3, sections 17–20.

CHAPTER 11

Paul: Background and Mission Call

No early Christian was as educated, cultured, widely traveled, visible, controversial, or intense as Saul of Tarsus, who became the apostle Paul. He was not among the disciples of Jesus—he never claimed that he saw the earthly Jesus—but he became Jesus' most visible and outstanding apostle and missionary. His life was marked by radical changes, from the very Roman city of Tarsus to the very Jewish city of Jerusalem; from radical Jew to radical Christian; from persecutor to persecuted; from imprisoner of others to prisoner; and from faith in the law and circumcision to faith in the grace of God through Jesus Christ.

Paul's life appears, at first look, very different from Peter's, but beneath the surface differences they shared several life-changing happenings. Like Peter, Paul underwent a change of name.[1] To both God gave life-changing insight into the true identity of Jesus as the Christ.[2] Both were led by the Holy Spirit to exchange their narrow ethnic view of God for a view that God's rule would stretch to cover every culture and people group. Finally, according to early Christian tradition, both were martyred for the cause of Christ in the city of Rome.

Paul's background, context, and talents

Paul was born and spent his early years in Tarsus, chief city of the Roman province of Cilicia (in modern Turkey). Tarsus grew increasingly important during the time that Greek culture dominated, and continued to do so after the Romans took over. Famous visitors to Tarsus before Paul's day included Alexander the Great, Cicero, Julius Caesar, and Mark Antony and Cleopatra. In addition to its Roman government headquarters, Tarsus was a center for trade and for higher education. Some time before Paul's birth, the emperor granted Roman citizenship and freedom from taxes to the residents of Tarsus.

Paul absorbed some of this cultural heritage of his home region. In his speech to the Areopagus (Greek court) in the city of Athens, cultural and intellectual center of the Greek world, he quoted the phrase "we are his offspring" (Acts 17:28) from a widely known poem by his fellow Cilician, Aratus, whose birthplace was not far from Tarsus. It is likely that as a young schoolboy in Tarsus, Paul knew about and was influenced by speeches and letters of the Roman proconsul and orator Cicero, who had once governed Cilicia, of which Tarsus was the capital. At the other end of the social spectrum, the boy Saul probably mixed with neighboring indigenous Turkish residents and was exposed to their language. This gave him insight into the more low-profile local cultures that would prompt his sympathy for them as future missionary.

Did Paul marry? The Bible does not answer this question, and his only mention of his own marital status was to state in passing that he was not married at the time he wrote 1 Corinthians: "Unmarried . . . as I am" (1 Corinthians 7:8, NKJV). He would have inherited from his Jewish culture a positive attitude toward marriage; after all, it was the focus of much of the Creator's attention according to the Genesis Creation story. Most Christian leaders in Paul's day were married (1 Corinthians 9:5), including Priscilla and Aquila, Peter, and Philip.

Paul was also highly educated. Peter and his fellow disciples had little or no formal education; Peter and John were seen by the Jerusalem temple authorities as "unschooled, ordinary men" (Acts 4:13). In contrast, Paul "studied under Gamaliel and was thoroughly trained in the law" (Acts 22:3). Gamaliel was one of the most respected rabbis of his generation, one of only seven in ancient Jewish society awarded the title *rabban*, "our rabbi."

Paul's education set him apart from Jesus' disciples and gave him a wider perspective on the world. His formal education probably started in a synagogue school in Tarsus, where he, along with other Jewish boys, learned to read the Hebrew Scriptures. The young Paul was then sent to Jerusalem to study under Gamaliel. This deepened his insight into the Hebrew Scriptures and their interpretation. He would need this when, after his conversion, he carried out the mission of establishing and integrating groups of believers made up of Jews, Gentiles sympathetic with Judaism, and Gentiles with little or no previous encounter with Judaism.

Also, when Paul declared, "I was born a citizen" (verse 28), he revealed an important part of his life. As a Roman citizen, Paul would have felt more secure on his journeys. Travel had become safer and easier under the *Pax Romana,* the stability and security brought to much of the Roman Empire by Emperor Augustus. Paul traveled widely and frequently. His missionary journeys recorded in the New Testament took him to eleven countries, twelve if he managed to reach Spain. The approximate total distance covered in these journeys was 15,500 miles (25,000 kilometers).[3] This feature of his ministry was vital for the rapid spread of Christianity.

Roman citizenship sometimes, but not always, sheltered Paul from rough treatment when he was brought before city magistrates. At times he could make use of his citizenship privileges to bring the gospel to a wider public than he otherwise could have reached. This happened in Philippi, where city rulers had to publically apologize to him for wrongfully imprisoning him, a Roman citizen (Acts 16:35–39). In Jerusalem his Roman citizenship won for him a chance to share the gospel with an angry mob attempting to kill him, while he was surrounded by protective Roman soldiers (Acts 21; 22). In other places, however, either his Roman citizenship or his Jewishness could have been a major obstacle. Today's missionaries need to have their national origin and citizenship carefully matched so they will fit into the target country with a minimum of risk.

And we cannot forget that Paul was a Pharisee as well. Pharisees made up a Jewish reform movement working to restore among the Jewish people respect for God's special laws, which they felt were neglected by ordinary Jews and even by the priests. The Pharisees influenced the Jewish people mainly in the synagogues, where the people gathered for Sabbath worship and where schools were located. Pharisees had little confidence in high priestly circles, whom they saw as little more than political figures appointed and controlled by Rome in order to help subdue and govern the Jewish nation.

Pharisees were on a mission to restore personal and national purity before God and to get the Jewish nation back to the way of life called for in the laws of Moses, so that God could fulfill His promises to Moses, repeated by the prophets: freedom from control by Gentiles, and restored prosperity for the nation (see Leviticus 26; Deuteronomy 28; Isaiah 54).

The Pharisees encouraged ordinary Jews to strive for the level of purity that the laws of Moses required of the priests.[4] For Pharisees, the laws of Moses included not only what was written in the first five books of the Hebrew Scriptures, but also the oral instruction that God spoke to Moses and which he passed on to Israel's elders, and by them to each following generation. Pharisees were "pharisaical" because they believed God wanted them to be that way—they wanted to obey and please Him.

But they were pharisaical for another reason. Groups of people quite naturally develop identity markers. Some markers need to be highly visible, to make it easy to identify group members. Special clothing and grooming can mark group members, as can rules about what is and is not taken into the body, such as food and drink. Special public rituals make group members plainly visible. This human tendency can help explain why some Pharisaic rules and regulations went well beyond God's own requirements for Israel, laid down in the Hebrew Scriptures.

Also, for Pharisees, proper Sabbath keeping was part of God's means of restoring Israel. Their attempt to limit Sabbath activity in order to prevent work on the day was the surface reason for several confrontations between them and Jesus.[5] The main point of the Sabbath commandment was for Israel to set the seventh day apart by having a break from their usual labor, trade, occupation, or craft that they did during the working week: "Six days you shall labor and do all your work" (Exodus 20:9).[6] Only by putting aside their own work, worries, and plans could the Israelites properly remember God as Creator of heaven and earth and receive the blessing that God put into the Sabbath day (verse 11).

Some Sabbath keeping practices demanded by the Pharisees had no support from the Sabbath commandment. These extra practices became a source of conflict with Jesus, who knew that God permitted people to "do good on the Sabbath" (Matthew 12:12). As a Sabbath keeping Pharisee, Paul (when he was Saul) would have emphasized strictness, as he says in his own description to King Agrippa: "I conformed to the strictest sect of our religion, living as a Pharisee" (Acts 26:5).

For the Pharisees, a boundary marker was to avoid eating with non-Jews in order to avoid losing purity. Table fellowship was especially difficult for a Jew if he suspected that the food on the table had been offered to a pagan god at a temple before it was put on sale in the market (1 Corinthians 8; 10:19–22; Revelation 2:14, 20). When Peter during his visit to Antioch stopped eating at the table with Gentile believers after Jewish believers arrived from Jerusalem, Paul rebuked him in front of the others: "Before certain men came from James, he [Peter] used to eat with the Gentiles. But when they arrived, he began to draw back and separate himself from the Gentiles because he was afraid of those who belonged to the circumcision group" (Galatians 2:12).[7] Even though Peter had pioneered the gospel to Gentiles, Paul was ahead of Peter in living out the truth that "God accepts from every nation the one who fears him and does what is right" (Acts 10:35).

Paul's conversion and missionary calling

Both the Hebrew and Greek words translated "to convert" in the Bible mean "to turn." So conversion is a twofold turning: turning away from what cannot save, and turning toward what can. Biblical conversion happens inwardly as well as outwardly. The biblical word for the inner part of conversion is *repentance*—a change of heart, intention, and will. God then empowers a person for the next step of conversion, the outward change of life's practices and habits, "repentance that leads to life" (Acts 11:18).

Paul's Damascus road experience followed this pattern. First, he repented—allowing the Spirit of God to change his mind about the direction of his life. He suddenly could see that his life as a persecutor was unacceptable to God.[8] Next, he turned away from his ungodly views, values, and actions and turned toward new ones. He followed Jesus' directions to get up, go to Damascus, and wait for further directions (Acts 9:6–20). As he declared later to King Agrippa: "I was not disobedient to the vision from heaven" (Acts 26:19).

All major features of the life of Saul of Tarsus—Roman citizenship, Jewish childhood in Tarsus, exposure to indigenous Turkish culture in his childhood neighborhood, Jerusalem education, commitment to the Pharisees, knowledge of the Hebrew Scriptures, witness of Stephen's stoning, life as persecutor—were transformed and put to work in Paul the apostle, evangelist, and missionary.

The lesson for Tuesday points out the five results of authentic mission work (verse 18).

First, to open peoples' eyes. As a Pharisee, Saul believed his eyesight enabled him to spot the truth and its enemies, the followers of Jesus. But God opened Saul's eyes, showing him a brighter light than he was currently familiar with: "I saw a light from heaven, brighter than the sun" (verse 13). In that light God appeared to Saul: "I have appeared to you" (verse 16). God then took away Saul's previous, defective spiritual eyesight: "The brilliance of the light had blinded me" (Acts 22:11). Saul "could see nothing"; "for three days he was blind" (Acts 9:8, 9); Then God, through the believer Ananias, brought Saul renewed, improved sight: "Brother Saul, receive your sight!" (Acts 22:13). "Something like scales fell from Saul's eyes and he could see again" (Acts 9:18). Saul's new spiritual vision was not for him to keep to himself. He was to share it: "Witness to all people of what you have seen" (Acts 22:15).

Second, "turn . . . from darkness to light." Saul was surrounded on the Damascus road by a new and brighter light, showing him that his life up to that moment had been darkened by wrong beliefs about the meaning of the life and crucifixion of Jesus. After three days of blindness in Damascus (Acts 9:9), Saul had his eyes opened even more during the visit by Ananias. Saul's own move from darkness to light inspired his mission.

Third, "turn . . . from the power of Satan to God." Satan's power over people shows itself in his ability to make people believe lies and disbelieve truth. The first satanic lie came early in human history, in the Garden of Eden, through the words of the snake that declared to Eve, "You will not certainly die" (Genesis 3:4). This denial of the reality of death, which is the belief that the soul continues to live after the death of the body, allows Satan to exercise destructive power over many people, keeping them in darkness about God's coming solution to the great curse of death.

Fourth, "receive forgiveness of sins." According to Paul's account of his conversion, Ananias ended God's message to the blind Saul with the instruction: "Get up, be baptized and wash your sins away" (Acts 22:16). Through the words of Ananias, Saul heard the words of Jesus, who in His ministry showed the power to forgive sins and free people from sin's crippling power (Luke 5:18–24).

Fifth, "receive . . . a place among those who are sanctified." The profound gospel truth expressed here is that persons who through faith in Jesus have their spiritual eyes opened, who have turned to the light of the gospel and from the grip of Satan's power and whose sins are forgiven, have an assured place among believers. There should be no restrictions created by ethnicity, gender, age, nationality, or economic standing. This was Paul's mission message, and it should be ours.

Paul in the mission field

As Paul adjusted to his newfound belief in the risen Jesus, and his call and commission to mission in the name of Jesus, he probably did not foresee that Jerusalem would cease to be his home base. He probably didn't think that he would spend most of the rest of his life away from Jerusalem, and that the Jerusalem-based urge to silence and kill the followers of Jesus, which had previously controlled him, would one day be directed against him. Thus returning to Jerusalem would become unsafe.

The Syrian city of Antioch on the Orontes River (not to be confused with Antioch in Pisidia of Acts 13) became Paul's adopted home base. Established about 300 B.C., it was the third largest city in the Roman world after Rome itself and Alexandria in Egypt. While the Jews made up a good-sized community in the city, they were not influential enough to stop the growth of Christianity, and there is no report that they troubled Paul. Antioch was the first city where the Christian message had been proclaimed directly to Gentiles (Acts 11:20), and where the name *christianos,* "Christian," meaning "follower of Christ," "Christ partisan," was first applied to the disciples of Jesus (verse 26).

Mission and the challenge of multiculturalism

The first "General Conference session" is the subject of Acts chapter 15. It had a single agenda item: circumcision.[9] As we already saw, the goal of the session was to decide whether the large number of Gentiles responding to Christian mission had to take on the full Jewish culture of the original Jewish believers. Some said yes, others no. The council decided, after much debate, that Gentiles did not have to undergo circumcision and similar Jewish cultural practices in order to become Christians. Word of this decision was spread to the mission field, especially Antioch, by the returning delegates (verses 22–29). The same Holy Spirit so clearly leading the way on the day of Pentecost, and in the home of Cornelius, worked during the session to confirm the rightness of the decision: "For it has seemed good to the Holy Spirit and to us to lay on you no greater burden than these necessary things" (verse 28, NKJV).

Conclusion

This week's lesson traced Saul of Tarsus from his Jewish origin in a prominent Roman city, through his life as a strict Pharisee and his fanatical persecution of the followers of Jesus, to his conversion and discovery that the good news of the gospel was for persons from all nations and ethnic groups. Paul the Pharisee, avoiding contact with

Gentiles for fear of contamination, became a fearless missionary to Gentiles, proclaiming Jesus to them in language they understood and freeing them from the Jewish cultural regulations that were not an essential part of God's will for all people.

---

1. From Simon to Peter (Matthew 16:16); from Saul to Paul (Acts 13:9). Peter is named about seventy times in Acts. The name Paul occurs about 180 times.

2. Peter could confess, "You are the Messiah, the Son of the living God" (Matthew 16:18). After Paul's Damascus road experience he confessed, "Christ Jesus my Lord" (Philippians 3:8).

3. Eckhard J. Schnabel, *Paul the Missionary: Realities, Strategies and Methods* (Downers Grove, IL: IVP Academic, 2008), 122.

4. René Gehring, *Die antiken jüdischen Religionsparteien: Essener, Pharisäer, Sadduzäer, Zeloten und Therapeuten* [The Ancient Jewish Religious Parties: the Essenes, Pharisees, Sadducees, Zealots, and Therapists] (Sankt Peter am Hart, Austria: Seminar Schloss Bogenhofen, 2012), 47, 499–516.

5. Gehring, *Die antiken jüdischen Religionspartien*, 517–530.

6. This is the focus of the two Hebrew words translated "labor" and "work" in Exodus 20:12, *'ābad* "to work, to toil, to serve" and *měla'kāh* "business, handiwork, craftsmanship."

7. There is a very useful description of the topic of group boundary markers, described as preserving identity, in Sigve Tonstad, *The Lost Meaning of the Seventh Day* (Berrien Springs, MI: Andrews University Press, 2009), 165–170.

8. "I persecuted the church of God" (1 Corinthians 15:9); "how intensely I persecuted the church of God and tried to destroy it" (Galatians 1:13).

9. Circumcision is today on a number of national agendas in Europe, partly due to Muslim and Jewish practices, and partly for possible health reasons.

Paul: Mission Theology and Practice

No early Christian was better prepared culturally, intellectually, and spiritually for world mission than was Paul. His knowledge of both Jewish and Gentile culture, sketched in the previous chapter, helped him become "all things to all people" so that he could win some for Christ (1 Corinthians 9:22). But the source of energy for his mission was not culture, intellect, or spirituality; rather his encounter with the crucified and living Christ, the Son of God, gave energy to his life and inspired him to proclaim Christ as the center of God's plan for saving humanity.

This week's lesson explores Paul's mission theology and his mission practice. The two were woven together like threads in a piece of cloth. Together they created a mission approach that joined sound theology to informed and open-eyed practice.

Paul's mission theology

Paul's mission theology belongs to what Seventh-day Adventists call the plan of salvation, the story of redemption, or the great controversy between Christ and Satan. Another label for Paul's mission theology is "salvation history." This is the belief that God has worked in different ways through history to bring salvation to humans. He sometimes uses even persons who seem unsuited, such as the pagan kings Nebuchadnezzar of Babylon (Jeremiah 43:10; Ezekiel 26:7) and Cyrus of Persia (Isaiah 44:28–45:6). Entire nations, such as Babylon (Daniel 1:1, 2) and even Rome (Romans 13:1–7), are revealed as among God's salvation agents when viewed through the lens of salvation history. The center of salvation history is Jesus, especially His crucifixion and resurrection, His service as heavenly high priest, and His return in power and glory at the end of this age.

Who can experience God's salvation as God's people? Paul's mission theology included the good news that, in Christ, no one would be excluded from God's people because of their nationality, ethnicity, social rank, or gender: "The gospel . . . is the power of God that brings salvation to everyone who believes" (Romans 1:16). "There is neither Jew nor Gentile, neither slave nor free, nor is there male and female, for you are all one in Christ Jesus" (Galatians 3:28).

Paul could not keep this good news to himself. Such liberated and liberating good news had to be shared. Paul's mission theology powered his mission practice: "I am compelled to preach. Woe to me if I do not preach the gospel!" (1 Corinthians 9:16).

Paul's mission practice

The example of a self-sacrificing Jesus motivated much of what Paul did. As Jesus had to live without the security and satisfaction of home and family, so did Paul. As Jesus moved around the territory that God assigned, so did Paul. In their mission practice both Jesus and Paul worshiped in the synagogues, inviting Jews and believing Gentiles to spread the good news about Jesus. Because of the controversy that followed their claims, both became unwelcome in synagogues and had to meet with believers elsewhere. Jesus met His followers in the open country of Galilee and in villages, the settings in which He had been brought up. Paul led believers to private homes and public meeting halls, where he continued his city missions.

Jesus rarely entered Gentile territory, working rather with "the lost sheep of Israel" (Matthew 15:24). He instructed His disciples on their first mission to do the same (Matthew 10:5, 6). Paul, on the other hand, was commissioned to take the gospel to Gentiles, as well as to Jews: "This man is my chosen instrument to proclaim my name to the Gentiles and their kings and to the people of Israel" (Acts 9:15).

Paul made use of all the resources available for mission. He traveled by land and sea, and he wrote letters that were read aloud and then shared with believers in other cities. By the use of letters, Paul, like Peter, was able to extend his mission into times and places where he could not be present. Along with the four Gospels, Paul's letters provide a permanent yet portable source for the message of Christianity. Along with the rest of the New Testament, they remain the church's most authoritative and inspired source for Christian belief and practice.

Paul's missionary messages

In order to understand the shame attached to a crucified person in the Roman world, one must first "switch off" the image of the cross and of crucifixion that has reached us through centuries of Christianity. Crucifixion was a public, brutal, and shocking form of Roman punishment for criminals and those who rebelled against the state. It was used especially as a punishment for "troublesome" slaves.[1] The sight of a crucified person generated feelings of revulsion, loathing, and fear. Crucifixions served as warnings to passersby to avoid upsetting the government. Passersby did not get the sense that the crucified person was suffering for the crime of another, but for their own crime. To Romans, crucified persons had only themselves to blame for their terrible punishment.

For Jews, the sight of a crucifixion brought to mind one of the harsher passages in the law of Moses: "Anyone who is hung on a pole is under God's curse" (Deuteronomy 21:23). This explains why Saul, before his conversion, violently opposed the claim of Jesus' followers that He was alive. To him, Jesus' crucifixion was evidence that He had seriously displeased God, and that He had come under God's curse, probably for His blasphemous claims to be the Messiah. But the risen Christ's appearance to Saul on the Damascus road opened his spiritual eyes and convinced him not only that Jesus was alive, but that He was the one He and His disciples declared Him to be—God's Messiah.

Saul realized Jesus was not crucified for His own sinful rebellion but for everyone else's—including that of Saul, the Jewish people, and the entire human population. Saul's transformed understanding of Jesus' crucifixion became the center of this message: the crucified Christ was no criminal but God's power and God's wisdom for the world (1 Corinthians 1:23, 24).

Paul's models for Christian life

How should first-generation Christians live? How could Paul and the other missionaries explain to new converts just the sort of life that was expected and required? They produced lists of specific "dos and don'ts," but such lists can never cover all possible life situations, and they can give the impression that the Christian life is nothing more than a list of those dos and don'ts. Leaders could also draw on abstract theological concepts to fill out their description of Christian life, such as devotion, loyalty, faithfulness, and persistence. But such concepts need to be brought down to earth in order to communicate their message. They need, so to speak, to be given feet and hands and faces that people can recognize and from which they can learn. To do this, models are needed.

Early Christian leaders used models for the Christian life that were well known and easily understood. Two of Paul's preferred models were athletes and soldiers. Both were widespread in Paul's world, and highly visible. Athletes displayed their skills in an almost unending series of contests at local, national, and international levels. One secret of their success was devotion to training and competing. For them, winning the prize was worth whatever it cost. The athlete's devotion to an earthly prize was a ready-made model for early Christian devotion to faith and to Christian standards. Those who persisted in the face of opposition and persecution would win God's heavenly prize in Christ Jesus (Philippians 3:14). Paul's athlete model would inspire his converts to persist until they reached the goal and won the prize.

It was common in Paul's world to see troops of soldiers on the streets and highways, stirring the emotions of onlookers. The presence of soldiers usually signaled peace and security, at least in places not in rebellion against Rome. Paul drew on the soldier as a model of loyalty, endurance, discipline, and readiness for battle.

The gladiator, however, was not suitable as a model of Christian life. Gladiators were not soldiers; they were solitary showmen entering the arena for single-handed combat. Unlike gladiators, soldiers worked in groups and were at their most effective when in combat formation, standing shoulder to shoulder, facing the enemy with shields held tightly together to protect themselves as well as the soldier beside them. Their famous Roman short swords were drawn and ready for whatever action ordered by their commander. This united, disciplined, and collective action provided a very helpful model for groups of believers (Ephesians 6:11–17).

Finally, soldiers were models for believers because they looked forward to receiving a reward, usually a tract of land along with a pension, at the end of their twenty or twenty-five years of service. Soldiers who were not Roman citizens when they began service could expect citizenship as part of this reward. Entire cities of retired citizen-soldiers sprang up across the empire. The city of Philippi was one. Probably retired soldiers were among the Philippian believers to whom Paul wrote that "our citizenship is in heaven" (Philippians 3:20).

Law in Paul's mission theology and practice

"Law" in the English New Testament usually translates Greek *nomos*, which for Greeks in Paul's day covered both formal law codes as well as what we call custom or traditional practice.[2] This calls for attention to the context whenever Paul referred to *nomos*. In some passages, such as Romans 2:17–25, he referred to the code of laws that God gave to ancient Israel. Elsewhere Paul used *nomos* to refer to the entire Old Testament, or to the five books of Moses. He used *nomos* to refer to one's customs or traditions in Romans 7:21–23 and 8:2.

The Ten Commandments occupy the central position in God's instruction to Israel. Written in a brief and direct "you" style, they spell out timeless, eternal principles governing a person's relation to God and to fellow humans. They are not limited to a single culture, or to time and place, but were woven into God's intention for humanity from the

Creation. This truth is made clear by their appearance in the Creation and Fall accounts, Genesis 1–4. Knowledge of the first and second commandments is assumed behind God's instruction to Adam and Eve about not eating from one tree in the garden (Genesis 2:16, 17). The seventh-day Sabbath was set aside for rest at Creation (Genesis 2:2, 3), and Cain already knew the wrongness of murder when he killed his brother Abel (Genesis 4:11). Cain broke another commandment, the one prohibiting false witness, when he denied knowing the whereabouts of Abel (Genesis 4:9). The permanence and ongoing authority of the Ten Commandments was brought to Israel's awareness when God wrote them on tablets of stone (Exodus 31:18; 32:16; 34:1, 29). These were placed inside the ark of the covenant (Exodus 40:20; Deuteronomy 10:1, 2) in the Most Holy compartment of the sanctuary.

Many other laws given through Moses were to govern Israelite life in the land promised to Abraham. They covered worship, farming, finance, family and community relationships, trade, and health. Moses wrote these laws in a book, and he then instructed the Levites to place the book *alongside* the ark of the covenant rather than inside it (Deuteronomy 31:24–26). This showed their importance for Israel, but at the same time their difference from God's eternally valid principles, summarized by the Ten Commandments, stored *inside* the ark.

The Ten Commandments had a central place in Paul's missionary message (see the passages listed in the lesson for Tuesday, under point 4). But he understood that many of the other Mosaic laws could be fully obeyed by Jews only when they were in control of their own land, able to govern themselves, and free to operate their temple and priesthood without interference.

That time had largely ended for the Jewish nation by Paul's day. He knew about Jesus' prediction that both temple and priesthood would soon be destroyed, and that many Jews in the area would be deported (Matthew 24:1, 2). That devastating event would make many of those specific ethnic laws and rituals written by Moses in that book stored alongside the ark pointless and impossible to keep.

Sabbath sacredness

No passage in the New Testament transfers seventh-day Sabbath blessing and sacredness to another day. Three New Testament passages are often quoted to support transfer of Sabbath sacredness to Sunday. In Acts 20, Paul, having survived a nearriot in the city of Ephesus as a result of his mission success, returned to the city of Philippi in Macedonia, where he stayed until "after the Festival of Unleavened Bread" (verse 6). Here Luke used the Jewish calendar, since that festival was specifically Jewish.

A core feature of the Jewish calendar was the reckoning of the beginning of each day at sunset. So the term "first [day] of the week," when the Philippian believers came together, probably referred to Saturday night after sunset. To "break bread" at the start of all meals was Jesus' custom, according to Luke 24:30, 35. As is clear in this passage, the expression was not used to describe only the beginning of a communion service. That day, resurrection Sunday (Luke 24:1), was certainly not sacred to Jesus' two disciples, who walked far beyond a Sabbath's day journey when they traveled the seven miles (eleven kilometers) from Jerusalem to Emmaus. When they finally recognized Jesus as He "broke bread," it was to begin the ordinary evening meal to which they had invited Him.

Colossians 2:16, 17 has been studied at great depth and length in order to recover the context, but without scholarly agreement.[3] Verses 9–15 preserve one of the New Testament's most exalted descriptions of the person, nature, and function of the risen Christ. The expressions "in him" and "with him" occur several times, expressing how believers benefit from Christ's death, resurrection, and heavenly ministry. With such a powerful Savior, Christians have nothing to fear from the lesser powers that lurk in the cosmos. Paul in this passage does not mention the Sabbath and certainly does not call for a change from Sabbath to Sunday.

In 1 Corinthians 16:2, Paul asked that money be put aside at home for a special charity project. He does not refer to an offering at a worship service. The key Greek word in this passage, *thēsaurizō*, occurs also in Luke 12:21 and James 5:3 in the same sense, referring to persons collecting wealth in their homes. Paul urges the Corinthian believers to start saving early each week, on the first day, so their gift of money will be ready to send when he arrives.

Resurrection of the dead

Paul's mission message gave no support to the nonbiblical belief that the spirits of persons lived on after the death of their bodies. He was faithful to the clear message of the Creation story, that living persons were a combination of physical body made from "dust of the ground" plus the "breath of life," which God breathed into the body (Genesis 2:7). At death, the body returns to dust and the breath returns to God (Ecclesiastes 12:7). Like other New Testament missionaries, he looked forward to his own resurrection at Christ's return (Acts 17:18; 23:6; 24:15; Philippians 3:11).

Mission finance and team relationships

Mission needs finance, and frontline missionaries rely on support from established churches. Antioch believers financed Paul's missions to new territories (Acts 13:1–3). Once established, those new congregations were expected to support their missionary founders. Paul listed the support that he and fellow missionaries expected of the congregations they founded: food and drink for the missionary and his wife, and a basic salary that freed the missionary from the need to do secular work. He called these "rights" (1 Corinthians 9:4–6), and he based them on principles in the Old Testament (verses 8–14). Sometimes Paul held back from claiming these rights (verses 15–18), but he insisted that they remained a biblical principle.

Paul did not support established congregations making payments to converts in new areas. To the contrary, Paul insisted that new believers continue to earn their own living (1 Thessalonians 4:11; 2 Thessalonians 3:7–12), and he modeled this by earning his own living while visiting churches.

Paul's mission success depended on teamwork, and he named some of the reliable and self-sacrificing team members who made his mission possible. The tension on teams caused by travel, living in other cultures, sickness, religious opposition, and threats of physical attack sometimes made necessary changes to team members (see 2 Corinthians 11:23–28). When Paul dismissed John Mark from his team (Acts 15:36–41), the younger man's mission career did not end. Paul later wrote "Get Mark and bring him with you, because he is helpful to me in my ministry" (2 Timothy 4:11).

Conclusion

Results of mission work must have seemed meager to Paul and his team at times, and they sometimes battled discouragement (Galatians 6:9; 2 Corinthians 4:1, 16). After his famous sermon in Athens, for instance, only a few believed (Acts 17:34). There were many moments of discouragement, exhaustion, fear, and suffering. But Paul's gratitude for Christ's sacrifice on the cross, which made possible his own forgiveness and cleansing from sin, inspired him for mission: "Although I am less than the least of all the Lord's people, this grace was given me: to preach to the Gentiles the boundless riches of Christ" (Ephesians 3:8).

---

1. Martin Hengel, *Crucifixion in the Ancient World and the Folly of the Message of the Cross* (London: SCM Press, 1977), especially pages 51–63.

2. *A Greek-English Lexicon of the New Testament and Other Early Christian Literature*, 3rd ed. (Chicago: University of Chicago Press, 2000), 677.

3. For an excellent summary of why this passage does not refer to the loss of Sabbath sacredness, see Ron du Preez, *Judging the Sabbath: What Can't Be Found in Colossians 2:16* (Berrien Springs, MI: Andrews University Press, 2008) and Sigve Tonstad, *The Lost Meaning of the Seventh Day* (Berrien Springs, MI: Andrews University Press, 2009), 259–277.

CHAPTER

Must the Whole World Hear?

This week's lesson explores two very challenging questions faced by believers. First, what will be the eternal fate of the many people who do not know the God of the Bible? Second, is there salvation outside Christianity?

Several related questions need to be asked: does the name of Jesus need to be heard, and called on, for a person to be saved? And how much responsibility falls on individual believers to warn unbelievers of their need for salvation?

According to best estimates, only one person in three alive on the earth at this moment is Christian. In other words, 2.5 billion Christians today live among earth's 7.3 billion inhabitants.[1] Many of these non-Christians have probably not heard the Christian message, so they have little or no idea how to seek salvation in the name of Jesus. This is important, because "there is no other name under heaven given to mankind by which we must be saved" (Acts 4:12).

How can God, who is "not wanting anyone to perish, but everyone to come to repentance" (2 Peter 3:9), work with the non-Christian majority of the world's people? Will He be content to choose those who are to be saved from among the one-third who are Christians, while accepting the loss of the non-Christian two-thirds? How does God deal with this matter?

Christians have answered this question in four main ways, each of which receives attention in this week's lesson. They are labeled exclusivism, inclusivism, universalism, and pluralism.

Exclusivism: Are non-Christians excluded from salvation?

Exclusivism is the label given to the belief that only Christians, those who know about Jesus and who have made a personal faith commitment to Him, can be saved. All others will be left out of salvation. They will have no place with God and the saved in heaven and in the earth made new. Exclusivists find biblical support for their belief that knowledge of Jesus and Christian faith is necessary to be saved mainly from Acts 4:12, John 14:6 and 17:3, and Ephesians 2:12, 13.

The Westminster Confession of 1646, official doctrinal statement of many Presbyterians and other Reformed denominations, supports the exclusivist belief when it states that

> much less can men, not professing the Christian religion, be saved in any other way whatsoever, be they never so diligent to frame their lives according to the light of nature, and the laws of that religion they do profess. And to assert and maintain that they may, is very pernicious, and to be detested.[2]

The official belief statement of the Southern Baptist Convention, a large Protestant denomination in the United States, echoes this exclusivist view: "There is no salvation apart from personal faith in Jesus Christ as Lord."[3] Some of the forty-five thousand Christian denominations currently in the world are even prepared to preach and maintain that there is salvation only in accepting their particular Bible understanding and doctrines. But such strict exclusivism rarely appears in other Christian belief statements.

The pioneers of what would become the Seventh-day Adventist Church went through an exclusivist phase following the great disappointment of October 22, 1844. They referred to it as the Shut Door, from Jesus' parable of the bridesmaids whose lamps ran out of oil, and who reached the house where the wedding took place after the door was shut (Matthew 25:10). In the words of former General Conference archivist Bert Haloviak, "Most sabbatarian Adventists concluded that salvation was available solely to those who had accepted Miller's teaching that Jesus would return in 1844."[4] He notes that references to this early Adventist exclusivist belief disappeared from publications after 1852.

The pioneers during this time seemed to focus only on fellow North Americans to whom they had witnessed. They did not take up the much bigger question of the millions in lands not reached by Christianity. As Adventist understanding of mission later expanded to include the unreached around the world, inclusivism replaced the original exclusivism. This is clear from Ellen White's statement in *The Desire of Ages,* quoted on Monday's page of this week's Sabbath School lesson.[5] Some Seventh-day Adventists still believe and claim that there is salvation only for those who follow the Adventist message.

In summary, exclusivism is a strongly stated official belief of a few denominations and a weakly stated official belief of a few others.

Inclusivism: Willing unbelievers saved through Christ?

Inclusivism is the label for the belief that persons who live up to the spiritual truth that they have can be saved, even if they have not heard the name of Jesus and the key truths of the Christian faith. For example, the *Catechism of the Catholic Church* follows the famous exclusivist declaration "outside the church there is no salvation" with a statement supporting inclusivism:

> Those who, through no fault of their own, do not know the Gospel of Christ or his Church, but who nevertheless seek God with a sincere heart, and, moved by grace, try in their actions to do his will as they know it through the dictates of their conscience—those too may achieve eternal salvation.[6]

Such bold, stand-alone inclusivist statements are hard to find in official Protestant statements of belief, possibly because they seem to weaken the motive for mission as one of the main tasks of the church.

But Protestant theological literature contains arguments for inclusivism, and leading Protestant thought leaders such as C. S. Lewis and Billy Graham are quoted in support.

Neither exclusivism nor inclusivism appears in the Seventh-day Adventist statement of 28 fundamental beliefs. Lesson author Børge Schantz has written in an earlier publication: "In a well-organized and detailed set of 28 fundamental beliefs we find doctrines that deal with gospel proclamation, salvation in Jesus Christ, the investigative and final judgment, and the resurrections of both good and evil people. However, the fate of the billions of un-warned is untouched."[7]

All denominations whose statements have been quoted above, whether inclusivist or exclusivist, are involved in carrying out the gospel commission. But their motives for mission, their theologies of mission, and their goals for mission differ, influenced in part by their stand on inclusivism or exclusivism.

Universalism

Universalism is the belief that all humans will be saved. A key passage is Jesus' statement: "And I, when I am lifted up from the earth, will draw all people to myself" (John 12:32). Universalism offers an answer to the question of how a loving God and Creator could allow some people to enjoy His presence eternally while allowing many others to suffer eternally in hell. Universalists answer this theological question by rejecting belief in an eternally burning hell, while they retain the belief that human souls are immortal. God will not, they believe, destroy any human soul, but will transform each one, without exception, into the image of the resurrected and glorified Christ. This transforming process may include a limited period of discipline and suffering to cleanse away sin and rebellion, but no soul will experience the second death, or eternal hell.

While universalist belief is expressed with the support of a few Bible passages, the belief's main authority comes from certain early church fathers. There is, frankly, no credible biblical support for belief in the salvation of all humans. However, universalists make extensive use of the Bible in their arguments against an eternally burning hell.

Pluralism

In many parts of the world today, tolerance has developed toward widely differing lifestyles and in attitudes and beliefs in such areas as politics and religion. People are gradually gaining freedom to think and live according to their own convictions. This trend has been helped by modern travel, communication, and immigration. People are learning to tolerate neighbors whose beliefs and practices differ from theirs. This process has included a leveling out of differences among religions and the introduction of religious tolerance. This has sometimes led to the belief that no religion is superior to any other as a pathway to God and salvation. This is religious *pluralism*, the assumption that all religions contain enough truth for personal salvation. For religious pluralists, there is no motive to challenge the religious beliefs of others or to introduce them to new ones, because they can be saved if they are faithful to their own religion.

The unbiblical core of religious pluralism is a major theme of both the Old and New Testaments. From Abraham onward, the God of the Bible called people out of their worship of false gods and idols. He continually appealed to them to worship Him alone, to the exclusion of other gods. To the Hebrews at the foot of Mount Sinai God affirmed in the first and second commandments His requirement of their total loyalty. His people were not to mix worship of Yahweh with worship of any other god.

New Testament missionaries had the same attitude toward the false gods of their day. They proclaimed Christ crucified, risen, and present through the Holy Spirit as the only true Son of God and worthy of worship, and they called people away from the worship of false gods. This is clear in the apostle Paul's experience in the city of Ephesus, where the Ephesian silversmith Demetrius, whose business was threatened by Paul's mission, declared truthfully that "Paul has convinced and led astray large numbers of people here in Ephesus. . . . He says that gods made by human hands are not gods at all" (Acts 19:26).

Part of Paul's message to the Ephesians about the true God is preserved in his letter to them. Before they came to Christ, they "followed the ways of this world and of the ruler of the kingdom of the air, the spirit who is now at work in those who are disobedient" (Ephesians 2:1). This meant they were "without God in the world" (verse 12), and "separated from the life of God" (Ephesians 4:18).

A close look at Paul's messages shows that he did not attack the false religions of the Ephesians. Rather, he pointed out the "smallness" of false gods, how powerless they were to protect followers, and their failure to elevate followers' moral behavior or to give them hope, healing, and salvation. Paul at times drew on his knowledge of the religions of his hearers, using some of their features to make contact with people and create interest in his message of the true God. This was clear in his Areopagus sermon (Acts 17). He must have used this method in his city missions in Ephesus (Acts 19:9; 20:20, 21) and Rome (28:30).

Seven biblical truths about salvation, and the human response to God's call

There is an all-important part of human nature that must be taken into consideration in the study of biblical mission: the freedom of the human will to make real and significant choices. This freedom is acknowledged by all Christian denominations, but they disagree about the amount of freedom available to humans in their fallen condition.

More important than denominational beliefs, however, is the testimony of the Bible about the reality of human freedom. The biblical evidence begins with Creation, where God instructed the man to choose wisely from which trees to eat (Genesis 2:16, 17). God also allowed the man to choose names for the animals (verses 19, 20). By granting free will to humans, God accepted the resulting limit to His own power and knowledge of the future.[8]

Human free will survived the fall and expulsion from Eden. According to Genesis 6:2–5, humans exercised their freedom to choose violence. Later the patriarch Abraham chose to "believe God" (Genesis 15:6). Even after generations of slavery in Egypt, and forty years of wandering in the desert, freedom of choice was assumed when Joshua challenged the Hebrew settlers in the Promised Land to "choose for yourselves this day whom you will serve, whether the gods your ancestors served. . . . But as for me and my household, we will serve the LORD" (Joshua 24:15).

Jesus acknowledged human freedom of choice. He called for choices in His public teaching. Matthew 5, for example, records twenty-four direct commands to His followers, each requiring a choice. He also expected those He called as disciples to choose. He declared, "Follow me!" four times, according to Matthew: to Peter and Andrew (Matthew 4:19), to an unnamed disciple (Matthew 8:22), to Matthew (Matthew 9:9), to the rich young man (Matthew 19:21). The latter chose not to become a disciple. Jesus allowed him to make that choice and experience the result, revealing the important place of human free will and freedom of choice in the biblical plan of salvation. God calls, and He allows humans freedom to choose their response.

Responding to God's call to mission

Another way human freedom is necessary for mission is in the calling of missionaries. God on some occasions sent angels to conduct missions. A few times He even used stones to testify silently (Joshua 4:4–9), and Jesus declared that if His disciples did not testify, the stones would cry out (Luke 19:40).

But in God's core mission plan, humans are chief carriers of the message of salvation. In choosing humans, God took a risk because humans, even when committed to God's mission, make mistakes. One could say that God, in choosing humans as mission agents, limited Himself twice: first, by granting humans free will; then, again, by choosing humans for mission. God has clearly decided to save only those who freely choose salvation.

The Bible's story of God's mission plan has two stages. The first, from Abraham to John the Baptist, focused on the chosen people, an ethnic group, to model God to the world. They were to be a "light for the Gentiles" (Isaiah 42:6). The Gentiles would come to learn of the true God, who was blessing Israel. They would then learn of God's wish to save and bless them as well.

God's second-stage mission strategy is the "salt" method, named from the saying of Jesus: "You are the salt of the earth" (Matthew 5:13).

Jesus' followers would go out to the nations, becoming scattered thinly across the world, like salt sprinkled on food.

Conclusion: The whole world

How big is the world? To Abraham and his descendants, it was what is known today as western Asia, the eastern Mediterranean, and part of northeast Africa—a very big region, with dual cultural zones dominated by Babylon and Egypt. By the time of Jesus, the world had expanded to include part of northern and central Asia, India to the east, and all of Europe to the west. Rome was the power center and Greece the source of much of the culture. By 1700, the world had expanded enormously, now to include the Americas, eastern Asia, the islands of the Pacific, and Australia. Europe held the power. At each of these stages the task of the gospel commission—the good news, the gospel, to all the world (Matthew 24:14)—appeared too great for the limited human resources of the missionaries.

For early Seventh-day Adventists also, the challenge of the gospel to the whole world was too big to take on. They believed it meant they were to spread the truth of the Sabbath and the soon Second Coming to the various ethnic groups settled in the United States. But soon they understood that the message was to go everywhere, and the church is doing just that, witnessing to our faith in Jesus in almost every nation in the world.

But mission is not yet finished. Every Seventh-day Adventist should ask, "What is my personal involvement in God's last-day mission? Is He asking me to more effectively witness to my own family and community? To join the new opportunities for mission made possible by mass communication and the Internet? To work with immigrants and refugees who have settled nearby? To leave home and country and settle among another people to spread the gospel through direct contact with others?"

This book's final word on mission comes from Ellen G. White, writing while in Australia sometime between 1891 and 1900:

> The message of the soon coming of the Savior must be given in all parts of the world, and a solemn dignity should charac-

terize it in every branch. A large vineyard is to be worked, and the wise husbandman will work it so that every part will produce fruit.[9]

---

1. Statistics from Todd M. Johnson and Peter F. Crossing, "Christianity 2014: Independent Christianity and Slum Dwellers," *International Bulletin of Missionary Research* 38 (2014): 19.

2. *The Westminster Confession of Faith,* "Of Effectual Calling," X.I.18, 19, http://www.reformed.org/documents/wcf_with_proofs/index.html.

3. *The Baptist Faith and Message,* "IV. Salvation," http://www.sbc.net/bfm2000/bfm2000.asp.

4. Bert Haloviak, "Practical Theology," in Terrie Dopp Aamodt, Gary Land, and Ronald L. Numbers, eds., *Ellen Harmon White: American Prophet* (New York: Oxford University Press, 2014), 165.

5. For further information on the changes of Seventh-day Adventist and Ellen White views from exclusivism to inclusivism, see Børge Schantz, "The Limitation of God and the Free Will and Holy Ignorance of Man: Towards an Understanding of the Plight of the Unwarned," in Børge Schantz and Reinder Bruinsma, eds., *Exploring the Frontiers of Faith: Festschrift in Honour of Dr. Jan Paulsen* (Lueneburg, Germany: Advent-Verlag, 2009), 403–420. See especially page 407.

6. *Catechism of the Catholic Church,* part 1, section 2, chapter 3, article 9, paragraph 3, clause 847, http://www.vatican.va/archive/ENG0015/__P29.HTM.

7. Schantz, "The Limitation of God," 413.

8. This theme is explained further by Schantz, "The Limitation of God," 406.

9. Ellen G. White, *Testimonies for the Church* (Mountain View, CA: Pacific Press®, 1901), 6:289.